BEYOND DEATH

Cover Art by *Madhu*

BEYOND DEATH

The Undiscover'd Country

Howard Murphet

This publication is made possible with
the assistance of the Kern Foundation

The Theosophical Publishing House
Wheaton, Ill. U.S.A.
Madras, India/London, England

This book was first published in Great Britain under the title *The Undiscovered Country*. © 1984 by Howard Murphet

© 1990 by Howard Murphet. First Quest edition 1990
The Theosophical Publishing House
306 West Geneva Road
Wheaton, IL 60187

A publication of the Theosophical Publishing House, a department of the Theosophical Society in America.

Library of Congress Cataloging-in-Publication Data
Murphet, Howard.
    [Undiscovered country]
    Beyond death : the undiscovered country / Howard
    Murphet.
       p. cm.
    Previously published: The undiscovered country.
  London : Sawbridge Enterprises, c1984.
    Includes bibliographical references.
    ISBN 0-8356-0654-6 : $9.95
    1. Death. 2. Future life. I. Title.
129-dc20   89-40619
                                   CIP

Printed in the United States of America

Death—the undiscovered country, from whose bourn no traveller returns . . .

William Shakespeare
Hamlet, Act III, Scene 1

Contents

Foreword ix

1. Childhood, Church and Bible 1
   Parental Teachings 1
   The Churches 3
   The Bible 9

2. Wider Horizons 19
   The Bar of Reason 19
   Primitive People 20
   The Egyptians 24
   The Greeks. Socrates. Plato 27
   A Story from Plato 31
   The Mysteries 37

3. Travellers Returning 43
   Personal Investigations 43
   The Society for Psychical Research 54
   Sir William Crookes 64

Contents

4. From the Borders — New Approaches 73
   Deathbed Visions 73
   There and Back Again 79
   From the Living who Died Long Ago 88

5. From Those Who Went to See 95
   Mainly Theosophical 95
   Some Rosicrucian Concepts 113
   Through the Swedenborg Door 117

6. Spiritualism: Informed Views and Warnings . 132

7. There Is No Death 156
   The Search of Nachiketas 156
   Vedantic Window on Life and Death 159
   Where East Meets West:
       Christian Science 168
   The Tibetan Book of the Dead 173

8. Summing Up 189

Suggested Reading 199

Index 201

Foreword

This book represents one man's search into what many men have said and believed, from earliest times until now, on life's greatest mystery: death. Shakespeare rightly called death an undiscovered country for, though teeming millions have gone there, none seem to have bodily returned to report as, say, Marco Polo reported on far Cathay, and Columbus on the mysterious lands across the Atlantic.

But, since the days of the Bard, determined research has thrown some light on the age old mystery. Travellers have, indeed, returned from points beyond death; they have glimpsed the bourn, and told what they saw and heard and felt there. Researchers are collecting these experiences.

Moreover, other travellers, even though they went beyond the point of no return, seem to have ways and means of communicating back, and telling us something about our *post mortem* destination. Psychic researchers have been examining and analyzing this evidence for about a century.

How do the findings of modern parapsychology and psychic science compare with the time-honored religious beliefs of man, the traditional cultures of different ethnic groups? Then, apart from the folk beliefs of early peoples, there are the accounts of a few travellers of recent centuries who penetrated, while still alive, into the undiscovered country. These are people with specially developed psychic faculties. Their modes of "travel" have been named travelling clairvoyance, out-of-the-body journeys, seership, or clairvoyance and clairaudience on the inner planes.

The extent to which each investigator was able to explore the hidden land and describe, in our everyday vocabulary, what he experienced there, depended largely on the degree of his psychic powers, together with his cultural background.

When the intelligence reports from all sources have been brought together, can we feel sure that there is, in fact, an undiscovered country somewhere out there beyond the sunset of life on earth? If so, it is worthwhile to take the pieces of the puzzle and fit them together to form a reasonably clear picture of what to expect when we "cross the bar." This I have tried to do.

I do not claim that this comparative enquiry is definite. It simply represents an investigation, spread intermittently over a lifetime, by one who has always been intensely interested in the problem of death, and its meaning in a rational concept of life.

I believe this is the first attempt to bring the main teachings, intimations and empirical evidence together, compare them and find whatever common features there may be, thus providing some useful guidelines for the inevitable journey to come.

If it also provides a signpost or two pointing towards man's highest destination, so much the better.*

But its main purpose is to help that person, gen-

----

*The word "man" and the masculine pronouns are used in this book for convenience only and are intended to include women and girls.

erally known as the man in the street, to see life and death in a new, and possibly happier, perspective. If it does this, removing some of his haunting fear, and revealing death as really an old friend, the effort will have been worthwhile. For, as Francis Quarles said, "Death has no advantage but when he comes as a stranger."

1
Childhood, Church and Bible

Parental Teachings

Our first ideas and thoughts on the subject of death come usually from our parents. It is said that what we imbibe in the years of early childhood remains firmly with us through life as a mental conditioning. I do not think, however, that this is necessarily true, especially for an enquiring, critical mind.

My own first gleanings on the subject came from my mother, who was a sincerely religious woman. She gave me the fundamentalist doctrines of the Protestant Church which were, in essence, as follows.

After death we lie asleep in the grave until the Resurrection and Judgement Day. On that day we stand before God on His judgement seat. With Him is the Book of Life in which are recorded all our deeds, words and thoughts. If these accurate celestial records show that we have lived a good life, we are sent to join the people on God's right hand. Otherwise we find ourselves with the larger crowd on His left.

Those on the right hand are sent straight to heaven, a glorious city of white marble mansions and golden streets. There they live in eternal bliss. The unrepentant sinners on God's left are cast into a lake of fire and brimstone, where they will suffer eternal torment.

1

Knowing full well that I was a sinner, the awful prospect in store for me should have filled my small soul with terror. In fact, it did not. Perhaps I sensed that my mother did not, herself, quite believe the ancestral doctrine that she taught. And even my childish mind could see that it was not in keeping with certain personal experiences she often related.

For example, when her own mother died in Launceston, Tasmania, she was living miles away near the little village of Hagley. One evening she saw in the sky above a shining vision of her mother being taken upward in a company of angels. She knew then that her mother had died, and a telegram some hours later confirmed the news.

Moreover, often when a member of her family died some distance away, my mother would hear three knocks on the window. She believed that this was the passing spirit of the dead one informing her. Some time after these strange knocks would always come the news of a death—often a sudden, unexpected one. Apart from such psychic sights and sounds, she sometimes felt the presence of the spirit of a close relative, recently dead, standing near her.

But if all dead souls were asleep in the grave how could such things happen? As I grew older I taxed her with this inconsistency. She did not attempt to explain it, but clung faithfully to the fundamentalist dogma her own father had taught her.

Even so, many noble spiritual teachings were given me by my first *guru*, my mother. Some of them — God's omniscience, for example — I dropped as being quite irrational as I passed along the corridors of secondary school and university. Yet years later, in the garden of meditation and greater understanding, I discovered new facets of my maternal spiritual teachings and knew them to be gems of truth.

However, one of her teachings I discarded in my age of reason and never again embraced: the doctrine of the sleep in the grave, and the resurrection of the physical body. In my lifelong search through time-honored religious teachings, the evidence of occult investigation and modern research, as well as through some personal experiences, I have never found anything to convince me of the truth of this irrational, primitive dogma. But I have found traces of how and why the idea of the body's resurrection might have come about.

The Churches

Nevertheless, in this last quarter of the twentieth century, some Christian churches are still preaching the doctrine, albeit with a few variations on the main theme.

"Since the soul is the person himself," says one church, "when the person dies it is the human soul that dies. The spirit, being simply the life force that enabled the person to live, returns at death to God who gave it. Only God can restore the spirit, causing the person to live again."

Hell, this church teaches, simply means the grave. At the general resurrection mankind's common grave will be emptied of its unconscious dead. They will be brought back to life. Some will be sent to heavenly glory as spirits. But the vast majority will be brought back to enjoy life in a restored earthly paradise. Here, if they carry out God's laws, they will never die again.

But not all those raised at the general resurrection will find themselves in heaven or the earthly paradise. Those condemned at the judgement following the resurrection will "go into everlasting cutting off" — whatever that might mean.

Another church that teaches the sleep in the grave until Resurrection Day offers a different scenario for the resurrection and after. Not all, only the righteous dead, will be raised from death and given a new life. They, along with the righteous people still living on earth at the time, will be taken up with Christ to heaven. The unrighteous dead in the graves, together with the unrighteous living then (who will be killed immediately by the "brightness of Christ's coming"), have yet another thousand years of unconscious waiting in the grave. During that period the earth will lie torn and lifeless. The only being on it will be Satan, "in awful solitude," surrounded by the devastation of his handiwork.

At the end of the thousand years the wicked, who have been lying unconscious, or non-existent, supposedly where their bodies were buried or disposed of in some way, will be resurrected. They will then receive God's judgement followed by final destruction by fire. It seems rather a pointless exercise to bring them back to brief existence simply to dash them painfully into non-existence again for ever more.

Also at the end of the thousand years the earth will be purged with fire (could it be the same fire that annihilates the wicked?). The old earth will then regain its original Edenic beauty, become God's Kingdom and man's eternal dwelling place. Presumably, the righteous, who have been enjoying heaven for the thousand years, will be brought again to earth which will be like a second Garden of Eden — but this time without a serpent to tempt the Eves; God's laws will be obeyed, and all will live happily ever after.

The Protestant churches that follow the above script, with variations, are usually called fundamentalist. They are in the minority. The majority are the "mainstream" or "mainline" churches: Methodist, Baptist, Congregational, Presbytarian, Unitarian, Lutheran, Episcopal and the Church of England.

I contacted most of them recently to enquire their current teachings on the vital question of life after death. All those to whom I spoke stated that the church had no doctrine on the subject. The congregation was left to form its own opinions and beliefs, and these varied considerably.

A section of mainstream churchgoers subscribe to the old fundamentalist ideas of a general judgement for mankind at the end of the world. Others admit their ignorance in the matter, feel that it is a mystery on which the holy book says little, and that it is best left to God, with faith that all will be well.

But some of those who cannot accept the old primitive fundamentalist dogma, and can get no acceptable guidance from their church, read the secular books based on psychic research. In this way they perhaps gain some light and hope.

In fact, the learned theologians who produced the modern authoritative volume, *Doctrine in the Church of England* (1938), admit that the question of an after-death state that is intermediate, somewhere between earth and heaven, and the idea of a general day of judgement for all mankind, present such great difficulties that they, the theologians, cannot agree on the matter.

One Anglican bishop observed at a conference in 1952, "We have renounced the idea of hell, and we have lost belief in heaven, except as a desirable, but probably fictitious, residential neighborhood . . ."

Some churchmen have told me that they do not actually believe in life after death. Others have only a vague optimism about it.

It was no doubt to fill the gap that opened when the old dogmas were no longer acceptable to the modern mind that the "Churches' Fellowship for Psychical and Spiritual Studies" was formed. This, under a different name, with more emphasis on "psychic research," came into being some decades ago. It uses mainly the mediumistic, spiritualistic methods of communicating with "the dead." Some leading churchmen run the fellowship, and ministers of religion have been prominently active in psychic research. Their findings are similar to those of Spiritualism and secular psychic research, which we will consider later.

The Roman Catholic Church *does* have a doctrine on the question. This is drawn from the Bible, but bears traces of earlier and occult teachings. It is, perhaps to some extent, tempered by the psychic research the sons of the Church have carried out themselves.

After death, says the Roman Church, the soul goes through the Particular Judgement, and then is sent straight to heaven, purgatory or hell.

On the Last Day will come the Final Judgement when every man's life will be revealed to the world, and the whole plan of God's providence made clear. At the time of this final judgement each soul will be reunited with the physical body it left behind at death.

Heaven is described as a timeless ecstasy where, in companionship with God, we shall also have the companionship of those we knew and loved on earth — that is, if they, too, saved their souls. In heaven God's presence fills the aching gulf in our hearts, and there is nothing more we can desire. While, in a sense united with God, we continue to live as individuals — perfected individuals with none of the inner conflicts, frustrations and desires that pestered us on earth. Heaven is everlasting.

Hell is also everlasting. It is eternal misery. If people do not choose to love God, and die in a state estranged from Him, they have only themselves to blame for their doom of everlasting unhappiness, says the Roman Church.

Yet, one asks, how does this eternal punishment square with the Christian belief in a benevolent, merciful God who is said to love and forgive His enemies, as Christ taught and demonstrated on the Cross?

A propos of this, a learned and compassionate priest of the Church remarked to me, "I do not believe that the soul of any human being suffers forever in hell. That fate is reserved for Satan and his fallen angels." I wonder how many priests share this view? The Church does concede that "hell is a mystery just as heaven is a mystery."

Purgatory, found neither in the Bible nor in other church doctrines, is a place where souls suffer for a time. The purpose of the suffering is to cleanse them of their sins and prepare them for life in heaven. "We do not know," says the Church, "exactly what the sufferings of the souls in Purgatory consist in. What is certain is that they are friends of God and that they are happy to be in Purgatory so that they may go to God pure of sin, and so be ready and fit to enter His presence."

The souls going through the purification process in this intermediate place can, the Roman Church states, be greatly helped by the prayers of the living, and that it has been the custom of Christians ever since the earliest days of Christianity to pray for the dead.

However, those churches that teach the sleep and static condition of the soul until the Final Resurrec-

tion and Judgement do not, of course, pray for their
dead. But the Roman Catholic Church quotes a text
from the Old Testament, giving authority for the
practice. "It is a holy and wholesome thought to pray
for the dead that they may be loosed from their sins."
(Maccabees 12:46)

Prayer and ritual for the deceased have played
important parts in the religious customs of mankind
since the earliest times — Hindu, Egyptian, Chinese,
Parsi and others. We will see later in the book that
the practice is supported by the various schools of
esoteric knowledge because, the latter say, the dead
are aided by the vibrations of love and the thought-
forms of good will emanating from this earth. The
deceased are, by such positive forces, helped to rise
from the lower planes to higher and happier spiritual
states.

But while the Roman Catholic religion agrees with
the esoteric teachings in this, and in some other
ways, it is unlike them in the strange importance it
gives to the physical body for ensuring the soul's
immortality.

Why at the time of the Final Judgement should the
millions of physical bodies, the elements of which
have long since been incorporated in other forms, be
brought back to unite with the souls that once occupied them? And why should the souls need such a
reunion? They have, according to the doctrine,
existed somewhere on the inner planes for thousands
of years without the support of their physical bodies.

The Church *does* say that the resurrected body will
have some spiritual qualities, that it will be freed from
the restrictions and limitations of its material nature.
In other words, it is really a transmuted body. But
the souls have presumably existed in astral and mental bodies, made of finer matter, between death and

the Final Judgement, so why do they need a trans-muted physical body for immortal individual existence?

This presents a puzzle, and when doing a course of study with the Catholic Enquiry Center in Eng-land, I asked a tutor to elucidate the points, if pos-sible. His written reply said: "We do not know exactly how the spirit of man lives on in Heaven, Purgatory or Hell before the Last Day, when it is re-united with its body. We do know from revelation that the existence is certainly personal, so that one is conscious of oneself in a very similar way to the one in which we are self-conscious on earth."

I admired the humility and honesty of the reply, but it did not throw any light on the question of what role man's physical body is supposed to play in his soul's immortality. Perhaps, I thought, the clue to the origin of this doctrine, and the reason behind it, might be found in the Hebrew and Christian Bible, or in other religions.

The Bible

The writer of Ecclesiastics said: "For the living know that they shall die but the dead know not any-thing." Some people take this to mean that the dead have no existence. But its meaning may well be that the dead, when contacted by the living, seem to know nothing at all, or nothing worth hearing. This has been the experience of many spiritists in modern times, and was no doubt so among the ancient Hebrews.

Some of the Hebrew prophets, however, indicated their belief in a continuous existence of the soul after death. One wrote that death "must be regarded as a benignity for the righteous man but as a dread calam-ity for the impenitent whom it ushers to his own place."

After death, according to Hebrew belief, the soul went first to a place they called Sheol. This was translated into Greek as Hades, and it did have much in common with the Greek idea of Hades, a gloomy grey place where the dead lived on in a sleepy, semi-conscious state. It was not a place of punishment nor of happiness. Existence there was neutral, colorless, apparently without purpose or hope.

Ideas change through the centuries and, later, Sheol came to mean a place of punishment. Gehenna was, however, the name given to the place of everlasting torment — the lake of fire and brimstone that burned the souls in eternal flames. It was the prototype of the Christian Hell.

Some of the Hebrew prophets taught that there is a resurrection of the dead. Isaiah, for instance, said, "Thy dead men shall live . . . the earth shall cast out her dead." (Isaiah 26:19) Daniel puts it more fully: "Many of them that sleep in the dust of the earth shall awake, some to everlasting life, and some to shame and everlasting contempt." (Daniel 12:2)

This does not say specifically that the physical bodies of the dead will be resurrected, but the idea is strongly implied. The belief in physical resurrection is found in other ancient Semitic cultures and in modern Islam. It is seen also in the early religion of the Chinese people. And in their practices the psychological roots of the belief may be detected.

"It is a well established ethnological fact," writes J. J. M. de Groot in *The Religious System of China*, "that savage and semi-civilized man as a rule explains sleep, swoon and unconsciousness as due to an absence of the sentient entity from the body." (Incidentally, the occult sciences agree with this concept.) The primitive Chinese, de Groot explains, believed that the wandering invisible spirit may be made to return by shouting, howling and calling the name loudly. Such calling does bring back the spirit when the person is in sleep or a swoon or a trance. Sometimes the return is immediate; sometimes it takes hours, or even days.

"Primitive man, having witnessed various durations of insensibility followed, in many cases, by reanimation, on beholding a body lying in a state which we are accustomed to call death, would naturally confound its condition with other states of unconsciousness and infer that the other self might possibly return to it. He would still entertain this hope even when the body grew cold, nor would he relinquish it when decay sets in. The persistence of the insensibility would prompt him to make strenuous efforts to bring the soul back." And so — standing on some high vantage point — he would shout the name of the deceased, and beg or command the spirit to return. It was the practice in old China to do this calling of the spirit from a roof top.

Even if the spirit failed to come back to the body after prolonged shouting and howling, it may, the people believed, eventually return of its own accord. As this expectation and belief had a firm hold on the Chinese of ancient times, they tried in many ways to prevent the mutilation and decay of the corpse. It was important to keep the body in a fit condition to receive the soul again.

In the process of time, with the advance of civilization, the old belief in the after-death cohabitation of soul and body waned away. Even so, numerous practices arising out of the resurrection belief survived into modern times, together with the idea that the spirit of the dead lingers near the body and is somehow intimately connected with it.

The early Egyptians also, according to some texts,

seem to have had a belief in the resurrection of the natural body. But this soon faded away. E. A. Wallis Budge, translator of the *Egyptian Book of the Dead, Papyrus of Ani*, states: "We are nowhere told that man's corruptible body will rise again."

The practice of mummifying the body — a process which practically destroyed the natural body anyway — had nothing to do with any idea of its resurrection. The attempt to preserve the dead person's appearance had other, more occult, reasons which we will consider in a later chapter.

In the New Testament we find that Jesus, the Christ, did not give us much information about the undiscovered country beyond death. He taught that there is certainly a life after death. In that life man will reap according to his sowing on earth. For the righteous there will be eternal bliss in heaven, for the wicked eternal suffering in hell.

But we don't need to be psychologists to observe that the majority of people, like ourselves, are neither wholly righteous nor wholly wicked. So, if being unfit to receive immediate bliss in heaven, or deserving of damnation in hell, where do the majority of discarnate souls find themselves after death? Is there an in-between place? Jesus does not speak of any.

The Roman Catholic Church, as stated earlier, filled the gap with Purgatory, a reasonable concept, borrowed from older pre-Christian teachings. The other churches, in the main, seem to have been content to leave the gap. To them, if Purgatory was not mentioned in the New Testament, the direct Word of God, it is wrong for man to introduce it into the Christian creed.

For the average mortal, guilty of many errors, many sins of commission and omission, the key to the attainment of heavenly bliss is repentance and redemption. If he repents sincerely, and strives to live a righteous life, the grace and mercy of Christ the Savior will raise him up, and even though being far from perfect, he will reach heaven.

But if he has failed to look squarely at himself, admit his sins, errors, and humbly asked forgiveness before his death, what is his fate? It does not seem that he is given a second chance "over there." If he passes through the door of death, and comes to judgement an unredeemed, impenitent sinner, there is nowhere for him to go but to the bottomless pit. There is no intermediate place where he can strive to purify himself and work out his salvation.

Somehow this concept does not seem very reasonable to the modern rational mind, influenced, as it is, by a scientific climate of thought. Consequently, as well as atheists, there are many nominal Christians who have no faith in the reality of a hereafter. Even some of the clergy themselves are doubting the old Biblical concepts on this subject. And as the Bible is their only textbook on the hereafter and immortality, they seem lost.

The situation is not helped by the fact that the New Testament seems to support the old primitive notion of the resurrection of the physical body. In fact, the story of Christ's empty tomb dramatizes the old Hebrew teaching on resurrection. Yet, at the same time, it brings in some new elements and suggests deeper meanings.

The incidents of the story, for example, show that the resurrected body of Jesus, though it is the one removed from the tomb, no longer has the limiting attributes of the body that was three days earlier nailed to the Cross.

When Mary Magdalene saw the risen body of Jesus standing near her in the garden, she did not recognize him, but thought he was a gardener. And when on the road to Emmaus the resurrected Jesus joined two close friends, and walked and talked with them, they did not recognize the man they had previously known so well. Then at the end of the long journey he blessed the food they were about to eat, and suddenly they realized who their companion was. Then the body of Jesus vanished in a moment from their sight.

Some time later, when some of his former disciples saw Jesus standing by the lakeside as their boat drew into shore, they did not recognize the Master with whom they had trod the hills and fields of Israel for years. When he miraculously caused their net to be filled with fish, they realized who he was.

A body that can change its appearance so much, can vanish at will, can appear suddenly in closed rooms, is more like an astral body, a body of finer matter, more malleable by mind and will power than is the physical body. On the other hand, the resurrected Jesus ate physical food with his disciples — not an astral trait — and to prove to them that it was the same body they had known, he invited them to examine the marks of his crucifixion and to feel his complete solidity. Finally, this solid body that could handle physical things, could cook and eat fish, faded like something ethereal from their watching eyes at the Ascension.

Saint Paul writes of terrestrial bodies and celestial bodies, of natural bodies and spiritual bodies. He likens the natural or terrestrial body to a seed that is sown in order that the celestial or spiritual body may be resurrected from it. The old body is corruptible; the new one is incorruptible, full of power and glory. So, from his teachings, it would seem that it is not the old physical body that is resurrected, the physical being but the seed that decays in order that the celestial body may spring from it.

I could find no answer to these strange Biblical mysteries and seeming contradictions when I was a scriptural student in the schools and Sunday schools of my youth. But later on in life I gained some hints of possible esoteric meanings in the Christian resurrection story.

If great scriptural stories actually took place in time, they have a meaning at that level, but also an esoteric meaning at the mythological level. If they did not actually happen historically, they still retain the deeper meaning of the myth, and their purpose is to project that meaning.

An esoteric meaning of Christ's resurrection is that the Divine Mind has complete dominion over the body. When man's lower ego is finally crucified in the course of his spiritual journey, and his Divine Mind rises from its carnal, mortal tomb, he is able to exercise full power. The new man, thus resurrected, will be master, not only of his material body, but of all material phenomena. He will also have complete freedom to be on this earth or to move to other subtler zones of existence as he wills.

That the emergence of the Divine Mind (the Christ) from the lower self will in fact happen to every individual in the fullness of time is a teaching of the spiritual philosophy of India. But when the individual reaches this level (most of the teachings say), he will ascend, as did Christ, to radiant realms far beyond the dark earth.

But there was one great Indian sage-philosopher who thought otherwise. Sri Aurobindo of Pondicherry introduced a new concept. Man's evolution, he said, does not end at the point where he is liberated from the desire-bonds of earth. His purpose is not to escape from the earth, but to work for the liberation and emancipation of the whole human race. And when this is attained in sufficient measure, mankind, through its developed divine power over matter, will transform this earth into a place fit for gods, fit for the Life Divine. The Kingdom of God on earth will have come.

What Aurobindo aims at, writes R. R. Diwaker, one of India's great scholars, "is the divinization and simultaneous transmutation, not only of individuals as they are, but also of the very material of which they are made. The mental, vital and material stuff of which man is made today is sought to be transformed into a subtler, finer and nobler substance, capable of taking man's whole being to a far higher level of existence where pure knowledge, "great harmony and divine bliss shall reign supreme."*

These are noble concepts indeed. But what a long way off such a true Kingdom of God on earth seems! How many centuries, how many millennia, will it take for the Divine Mind of man to be liberated from the dark tomb of his desire-nature? When thus beyond the thraldom of nature, man will have the power to command and transform nature. But would he not choose rather to move into the realms of the blessed, the blissful heaven world?

In the Christian resurrection story, be it actual or symbolic, the resurrected Jesus ascended to the higher realms. But some say he is also here on earth, using a physical body with the same powers as his body of resurrection.

One of his main teachings was that, though the Kingdom of God is within us, it will also come into

---

*See *Mahayogi Sri Aurobindo* by R. R. Diwaker, Bharatiya Vidya Bhavan, Bombay, 1967.

manifestation on earth. But his followers thought he meant that it would come quickly, in the morrow of their day. Some are still expecting its early arrival.

The words of Jesus certainly seem to suggest that it would come within a few years of the time he spoke — two millennia ago.

But perhaps he was thinking in terms of God's time rather than man's. Time is only a dimension of measurement that changes at different levels of consciousness. That such changes can be vast is well illustrated in the story of an ancient Indian king who could not find a bridegroom he thought worthy of his daughter. There were many suitors but none met with the king's approval. Finally he decided to take his problem to Brahma, the creator of the universe.

Arriving in Brahmaloka, the divine abode of Brahma, holding his daughter firmly by the hand, the king found that Brahma was occupied in other matters (some versions say he was watching a dance). So the king and his problem princess waited. Within a few minutes, however, Brahma called him for an audience, and the king explained his problem, requesting that Brahma would solve it by selecting the right husband for the princess.

The God replied, "In the few minutes of our time that you have been waiting here a whole age has passed away down on earth. All the suitors for your daughter's hand have been long dead. Lord Krishna is now a divine *avatar* on earth, and his brother Balarama will make a good husband for your daughter. Hurry back and arrange it while there is yet time."

According to Hindu concepts, one day of Brahma is equal to 4,320,000,000 earth years.

I believe, myself, that the symbolic story of the empty tomb was in fact acted out in Palestine some two thousand years ago. By taking its surface meaning, some churches have created a confusing and hard to accept doctrine. If they would examine its symbolic esoteric significance, they might discern a sublime spiritual truth about man's destiny.

But when in youth I puzzled over such Bible stories any deeper meanings they may have were still hidden in the womb of time. They did not help in my search for the meaning of death.

It is a good thing to be born in a church, but a bad thing to die in it.

Sri Satya Sai Baba

2

Wider Horizons

The Bar of Reason

Science, logic, mathematics, anthropology, the classics and other subjects in secondary and tertiary education awakened my reason and widened my mental horizons. The old dogmas had to stand or fall before the newly found bar of reason. Most of them fell. There was no proof of life after death or the immortality of man, for instance.

The physics teachers of the time taught that matter was the only reality. It could be measured, weighed and analyzed down to its basic foundation: the atom. It could be converted into other forms of matter but it could not be destroyed. From matter emerged, by chance, life and consciousness. So where was there room for the soul? When the body died, its whole mental superstructure went with it. Though the generations might go on and on forever, like Tennyson's brook, the individual ceased to exist at death. This is the kernel of the materialistic philosophy to which I was exposed in the academies of higher learning during the 1920's.

Since then, of course, the edifice of materialism has been badly shaken. Its cornerstone, the indestructability of matter, collapsed with the first atom bomb. Matter, the solid basic reality, had been exposed as an airy fairy nothingness. It was mainly empty space.

If one atom could be expanded to the size of a football field, scientists say, its central nucleus of positive energy would be no larger than a green pea, and the negative electrons revolving around it in the great space would be even smaller. These primary elements of the atom are being broken down further and further into patterns of energy, and the behavior of the patterns is unpredictable and inconsistent. The rationality of science seems to be transcended within the atom. Perhaps, as Madame Blavatsky wrote in *The Secret Doctrine* last century, the atom is "infinitely divisible." At any rate, what we thought was solid matter is really only patterns of energy that act peculiarly and illogically in great empty spaces.

But such concepts were outside the smug, self-satisfied rationalism of the schoolmen of my student days. Disdainfully scientists and custodians of the new thought were sweeping away the cobwebs of the old beliefs.

Many of my contemporaries became atheists. I, myself, did not make this complete turnabout. Whether it was through early conditioning, or something else that lay deep within me, I do not know. I still believed in the possibility of a God, a life after death, an immortality for the soul of man. Dogmatic atheism seemed to me as unreasonable as dogmatic church doctrines. So I became an agnostic, a questioner, a searcher. I wore the cloak of scepticism, not because it was fashionable, but because it seemed a safer road to the truth than the old blind faith of theology.

Primitive People

"Steer clear of the bogs of superstition. Stick to the firm road of reason," said the philosophers of science. Yet to discard all the accumulated beliefs of thousands of years may be to throw out the baby with the bath water. Some worthwhile gems of truth may lie within the rubbish of superstition.

Enough primitive peoples have existed on the earth during the last century for anthropologists to study what such people, isolated from each other on different continents, thought on the question of life after death. Moreover, archaeology has been able to deduce from remains in ancient burial grounds what the early uncivilized peoples of some countries believed about the destiny of the soul.

It is interesting that practically all the primitive peoples throughout the world have believed firmly in a life after death. Their ideas on what the spirit of a dead man was like in nature, where it went and what kind of a life it lived, varied somewhat, but the actuality of *post mortem* existence seems to have been for them a matter beyond doubt.

The modern materialist may say that this primitive belief was born of wishful thinking. But such an explanation has little verisimilitude when we see that the primitive notions of the hereafter offered more gloom than pleasure. Their psychic intimations of the continued existence of their dead probably came from earthbound spirits, which a large proportion of the deceased savages seem to have been. Their apparent homeless existence in trees, caves, rivers, the sea, or hovering near their own burial place, was not an enviable life. Perhaps the deceased ones suffered hunger, thirst, or some other wants, it was thought. Perhaps they were angry and malignant because of their unsatisfied desires. Anyway, many primitive tribes were afraid of their ancestral spirits as children are afraid of ghosts.

The great anthropologist, Sir James Frazer, states

that many primitive peoples were afraid even to mention the names of the dead lest it invoke their spirits. The taboo on speaking the names of deceased persons was observed by some peoples in antiquity, and in modern times was found as a strict custom among the Australian aborigines.

In some of the tribes, if people were compelled to mention the dead person's name, they would do so in a whisper, hoping that the spirit would not hear it. Other tribes would not use the actual name even in a whisper, but employed such expressions as "the lost one" and "the poor fellow who is no more. "

The primitive fear of the dead is shown not only in such taboos, but also in the custom of periodically driving the earthbound spirits from the district with various rituals. Some of the Australian Blacks, for instance, annually expelled the ghosts of the dead from their territory. This freed the living from the malignant influences that had been accumulating, and they were able to make a fresh start. Some of the early Christian missionaries observed these yearly spirit expulsion ceremonies, which were accompanied by loud noises, pantomimes with gaudy decorations and battle actions against the unseen foes.

Such uncomfortable and trouble-causing folk beliefs would scarcely come from the psychology of wishful thinkers. Much more likely, the belief in life after death was born from direct psychic perception. It is well known that extrasensory perception is more alive and active in primitive than in sophisticated societies. The development of the rational mind and intellect in civilization seems to push the natural psychic sense of man into the background.

Many native people would no doubt feel, and sometimes see, the presence of the spirits of their departed, as a few rare psychic individuals do in civilized communities. The direct perceptions of the natives would give them sure knowledge of the fact of survival — unconfused by church dogma about the sleep of the soul in the grave.

In primitive African societies, before the influence of the Christian and Muslim religions, the dead were as real as the living. For many years after death, until they had faded from living memory, they were regarded as what has been called "the living dead." In a sense they were somewhere between those still in physical bodies and the spirits of the long departed who had gone into a more remote state.

To the African the continued existence of the living dead members of his family was a matter of direct perception. When one of them appeared to him, he was not altogether delighted; he did not give the spook a warm welcome. Nevertheless, he offered food and libations of beer, milk or water. Such symbolic offerings constituted a communion of fellowship with the living dead.

While not being generally afraid of their dead, as some other primitive peoples were, the Africans showed great respect, and were careful to carry out any instructions given, either by the dying person or by his apparition after death. Otherwise, they felt that the living dead one might be angry and bring them some kind of misfortune or disease. Furthermore, they felt that these deceased members, if treated well, would act as intermediaries between them and the high spirits, or with God.

After the last person to remember him, even by name alone, had died, the living dead one moved on into the realm of spirit. His death was now complete. His old appearance, name, and personal attributes vanished, and his personal immortality was over. This meant that he now became part of the community of spirits, and was no longer the concern of his family connections on earth. If the spirit now appeared, which was rare, it came as a stranger.

Professor John S. Mbiti writes in *African Religions and Philosophy*: "Belief in the continuation of life after death is found in all African societies, as far as I have been able to discover."

He goes on to explain that their hereafter is conceived in materialistic and physical terms. There is no hope for a paradise nor fear of a hell, no concept of spiritual progress. The highest state the common man can reach is that of a spirit. Only very rare spirits become associates of God, and there is no concept of union with the Divine. But the common spirit is able to communicate directly with God, and sometimes does so on behalf of living people.

The Egyptians

In Egypt the rich soil of the Nile delta has been for thousands of years surrounded by arid desert. Take a step from the alluvial soil, usually covered with the green carpet of three crops per year, and you are on the brown sands of the desert. But for over six thousand years these bare arid sands have had one excellent use. The Egyptian people have buried their dead and erected their funerary monuments there. Except where intentionally destroyed, the tombs, the items that were interred with the dead in their tombs, the mummies, the monuments, have all been preserved intact in the sands right up to the present day.

Among the thousands of tombs opened there, some date from about 4500 B.C. when the Egyptian race was emerging from the Stone Age. In those prehistoric burial places we can see signs of an unwavering belief in a life after death. This belief remained a prominent element in the Egyptian religion throughout its long history.

The early Egyptians, like other primitive peoples, thought that the souls of the dead stayed on, or very near, the earth. There was an underworld called Earu, close to earth, where the spirits of the dead lived. There they would need the same things they used in ordinary life. So along with the corpse were buried, or entombed, their implements, weapons, ornaments, and a full complement of household pots and pans.

Incidentally, this custom still survives among the people of the Libyan desert. During World War Two, I saw there the implements, clothes and other items in the stone dome-shaped tombs of sheikhs, and on the tops of the graves of the common folk. The custom may not now be inspired by the belief that the soul will need these material things in the hereafter. Old practices often continue long after their original meaning is lost.

The prehistoric Egyptians also had the idea that the dead may suffer hunger and thirst, so they made periodic offerings of food and other necessities. They were apparently not afraid of their dead as were some other primitive peoples. In fact, the Egyptians, very early in their history, had special places constructed above or near the tombs where they could meet the spirit and make the regular offerings.

As time went on their idea of man's fate after death became more complex. The changed concept incorporated the legend of Osiris. This great god-king had been murdered by his brother, but was eventually brought back to life by the love of his sister-wife, Isis. In his resurrected body, however, he was not able to resume his reign on earth. He became instead the king of the world beyond death.

It is interesting that this resurrection of the body of a king, taking place long before the resurrection of Jesus, did not lead the Egyptians to a belief in the final resurrection of all physical bodies, as in the Christian doctrine.

Put simply, what the Egyptians believed was that besides his *ka*, the entity that kept in touch with his burial place, man had also a higher spirit. This spirit had a glorified future life in the kingdom of Osiris. In some strange way, if buried with the proper rites, each person became Osiris. His higher spirit that took wings to the divine kingdom was called his 'Osiris.'

Some Egyptologists say that the preservation of the mummified body was of vital importance because the dogma of Osiris taught that from it would spring the effulgent, translucent envelope (body) which the spirit of the deceased would occupy, with all its mental and spiritual attributes intact.

A person's Osiris, or glorified body, consisted of all his non-physical parts gathered in a form that resembled him exactly. Furthermore, all honors paid to the physical body were received by its Osiris, or higher spirit. For the well-being of the dead one's spirit — the Osiris as well as the earthbound *ka* — it was necessary to preserve the natural body in the form of its mummy.

So, while from the beginning the Egyptians believed in a life after death, their ideas of it developed through the millennia. At first it was the single *ka*, requiring offerings of sustenance at the grave. Then came the plurality of spirits. The *ka* still remained at the lower levels, but the *ba* ascended to happier regions. Yet while it lived in the heavens as a glorified individual, keeping the form and appearance it had on earth, in some inexplicable sense it also became one with the divine Osiris.

This may seem a strange ragbag of ideas to the modern mind, but in its elements there are echoes and intimations of a great truth. We will see how ideas and concepts developed more fully later, through empirical evidence and deeper teachings, bear a relationship to the ideas of the ancient Egyptians. In other words, further reports coming in from the undiscovered country explain, amend, expand rather than contradict outright the earlier reports.

The Greeks, Socrates and Plato

Some ancient Greek notions about death were similar to those of the Egyptians, but their greatest philosophers came to a deeper understanding.

The Greek god of death, called Thanatos, was the twin brother of Hypnos, the god of sleep. It is natural for man to see a close relationship between death and sleep. But to the Greek the sleep of death was not oblivion. Rather, it was like a far from happy dream. The souls of the dead, after being ferried across the dark waters of the Styx by Charon, dwelt in a grey, gloomy, mist-filled place called Hades, the parallel of the Egyptian Earu, the Hebrew Sheol and other underworlds visualized by the primitives.

The inhabitants of Hades existed in a sleepy, dream-like state — pale shadows of their former selves. They had lost their intelligence and courage; they had no purpose, occupation or hope. Hades was a kind of dismal house of retirement.

Gradually, however, this primitive conception of the underworld changed, and it came to be considered a place of justice. Souls, on arrival there, appeared before a tribunal composed of Hades and his three assessors.

After judgement each soul received exactly what it deserved. The worst were cast into Tartarus; others were conducted to the Elysian Fields.

Tartarus was surrounded by a triple wall washed by a river. The avenue leading to it was closed by a diamond gate, while other gates were of bronze. This classical hell was a somber jail for evildoers, and especially for those who had committed crimes against the gods. The punishments were varied and terrible.

In the paradise of Elysium snow and rain and tempests were unknown. Soft breezes forever refreshed the souls of the just and good in these abodes of peace and happiness.

A few rare souls at death were elevated to Olympus where they dwelt eternally among the immortals they had worshipped. But to the common man, the average citizen with his many small sins, the hereafter held out more fear than hope. It was not an enticing prospect. Yet he had no doubts about its existence.

That great doubter, questioner, rational thinker, Socrates, felt sure too that the human soul lived on after mortal death. In prison, just before he drank the hemlock, he spoke dispassionately about his own imminent death, showing that his hopes were high for a life much better than the one he was losing.

"How shall we bury you?" asked his friend Crito. "Any way you like if you can catch me," he replied, laughing. "I can't persuade Crito," he explained to the others present, "that I am this Socrates talking to you now. He thinks I am the one he will presently see lying dead. My long and elaborate explanation that when I have drunk the poison I shall remain with you no longer, but depart to a state of heavenly happiness, seems to be wasted on him."

The young Plato, Socrates' greatest pupil, was present at the historic scenes before the Master's death. He describes them in his 'Phaedo.' Socrates, he says, was constantly cheerful in anticipation of his spirit being released from its prison, the body.

The ideas on death given by Socrates — whom the Delphic Oracle named the wisest man of his time — are worthy of study. He told his friends that when a man dies, his guardian spirit, which has watched over him during his lifetime, takes him to the place of judgement. Following the judgement he will be guided to wherever he is destined to go for the initial period of his *post mortem* existence. Incidentally, the Parsis also teach that the guardian angel of a person's life will be his guide in the transition to the next world.

The wise and disciplined soul, Socrates told his listeners, will follow the guide. But the soul that is deeply attached to the body, and to the pleasures that it has gained through the body, will hover around the visible world for a long time. Only after much resistance, and consequent suffering, can such a soul be led away from this world.

If during his life a person has kept himself free from the contamination of the lower desires, and been governed by love and wisdom, truth and justice, his soul will find itself soon after death in a place that is divine. Indeed, Socrates said, the pure soul reaches a place "where (as they say of initiates in the Mysteries) it really spends the rest of time with God." But the attainment of such a divine abode is only for the soul that is pure when it leaves the body.

Those who are judged to have lived a neutral kind of life — neither very good nor very evil — remain for a time in regions where they undergo purification. There they are gradually absolved from their sins through the sufferings of purgation — the prototype of the Roman Catholic Purgatory.

The souls whose crimes have been very great and terrible are cast into Tartarus. After a period there, a river carries them near a point where they can communicate with those who had suffered from their crimes. The souls cry aloud and entreat forgiveness. If they are forgiven, they are allowed to leave the river, and their miseries cease. If not, they are whirled off again by the current and must suffer the torments of Tartarus until, at some later time, they obtain forgiveness from those they have wronged.

Some, however, whose crimes have been horrible, revolting and persistent, have consequently sunk into such an evil-loving state that they are judged to be irredeemable. Such evil, unrepentant souls, once hurled into Tartarus, will emerge no more.

In order to have a good death and a happy hereafter, the old philosopher pointed out, man must live a good life. He must abstain, as far as possible, from those desires, passions and pleasures that rivet him to his body. Otherwise he will find it hard to get away to the unseen world of happiness after death. A soul too saturated with the call of the body will "soon fall back into another body, where it takes root and grows. Consequently it is excluded from all fellowship with the pure and uniform and divine."

Here Socrates touches on the idea of the transmigration of souls which some great thinkers of the classical world seem to have accepted as true.

Disclaiming any exact detailed knowledge of the great unknown country, the philosopher said: "Of course, no reasonable man ought to insist that the facts are exactly as I have described them, but that this, or something very like it, is the destiny of the soul after death."

He explains how difficult it is to obtain knowledge of reality by likening the human body to a prison. We think that we are perceiving reality through our five senses, but these, he says, are like slits in the walls of our prison through which we get only a distorted view, limited and false. When Philosophy (the lover of wisdom) tries to set the soul free, "she points out that observation by means of the eyes and ears and all the other senses is entirely deceptive." Only by looking inward to the invisible world can the soul see reality and know the Truth.

After Socrates had drunk the hemlock, and was waiting for the paralysis of death to creep slowly from his feet to his heart, he talked with a gentle, ironic solicitude to his sorrowing friends in the room. His last words may seem enigmatic but they were really quite clear.

"Crito," he said, "we ought to offer a cock to Asclepius. See to it and don't forget."

Asclepius, the god of healing, was about to cure the great philosopher with death, about to release his soul from the disease and suffering of its bodily prison. A sacrificial cock must be offered in thanksgiving for such a complete healing. This is the way one of the world's greatest men thought of death.

A Story from Plato

After the death of Socrates, Plato wrote some twenty-two dramatic philosophic dialogues. Socrates appears as the leading character in many of these. It is difficult, in fact impossible, to know which ideas were from the great Master and which were Plato's own.

The rational mind of the ancient Greeks is at its best in these two philosophers. With them it seems to have burst through old barriers of mental habit, and fanned out over new horizons. Yet Plato makes it clear that the quest for the transcendental truths of life and death must go beyond even these wider horizons of the logical mind. It must look also to the realms of vision, allegory and the higher intuitions.

The intimations we get from such realms may lead us towards the truth about life after death, for instance.

In Book X of *The Republic* Plato tells a story which I, along with most students, took to be an allegory. It may well be, but in the light of near-death experiences collected by researchers today, it may be a factual story. But even though an actual experience, some of its elements seem to be allegorical or symbolic.

After a great battle the dead were being gathered together for proper burial. All the corpses were found to be decomposing except one which appeared quite well preserved. This proved to be a soldier named Er, the son of Armenius. His body was taken, however, along with the others and placed on a funeral pyre.

But just before they disposed of his body, Er sat up on his funeral pyre. After the shock, fear, consternation and rejoicing of his relatives and friends had subsided, Er told them a strange story. He seemed to remember all that had happened to him during the days of his clinical death.

After he fell in the battle, he said, his soul had travelled in the company of others to a mysterious region. There he saw many souls brought in front of judges. He noted that on either side of the judges were sets of doorways or openings: two to the right and two to the left. Someone informed him that the doorways to the right led to the heaven worlds, one being an entrance and the other an exit. Those to the left — also entrance and exit — led to Tartarus.

As he watched the scene of judgement, he observed many souls being sent to the right and many others to the left.

After some time Er was brought, with great trepidation, before the judges. He was surprised and relieved when they told him that he was not for judgement this time. He was here as an observer. He must watch carefully, and when he went back to the life of the world, for he would be sent back, he must tell all he had seen.

So Er stood aside and observed the drama taking place on this bourn of the great hereafter. He soon noted that there was a stream of people coming from the exit doors on each side of the judges. They were obviously souls returning from both heaven and Tartarus. They mixed freely together in the great meadow where Er seemed to be. He walked among them and talked.

Some, who had come from the region of the damned, had spent maybe thousands of years of suffering there. An eternity, it had seemed to them. Some from heaven told him of the wondrous joys they had experienced there. Their rewards in heavenly happiness seemed to them to be ten times what they had earned.

Those from Tartarus described how often, when they had come near the exit, eagerly hoping for release, they had heard a mighty voice bellowing forth, denying them their freedom. They would then be sucked back into hell for further torment. Later, whenever they approached the exit, they were in great fear of hearing the stentorian voice. Therefore, it was a tremendous relief when finally they found themselves out of hell, as they did now.

They were camping on the wide meadow along with the souls down from the upper regions, and many stories of heaven and hell were exchanged.

After some time in the meadow, the whole company, Er included, moved off to another place, and all knew that from here they would be returning to lives on earth in new bodies. Er understood that he himself would be going back to the old body he had left on the battlefield.

At this take-off spot for the return journey to earth, Er witnessed another interesting drama. The whole company had assembled in front of Lachesis, the daughter of Necessity. From her lap a prophet took a pile of lots and tablets. On the tablets were inscribed patterns of earth lives that could be chosen. On the lots were numbers.

Standing on a high platform, the prophet explained to the assembly that their next lives on earth would be determined by their own choice, even though there was an element of chance in it. The lots would be thrown among the people, and each must pick up the lot that rolled nearest his feet. The number on his lot would determine his order in the queue for choosing a new life. Number one would have first choice and so on, according to numbers held, until all had chosen.

But no one should worry about what number fell to him because everyone would have the opportunity to choose a good life: there would be more life patterns on show than there were people in the gathering. The main thing was to choose with great care and discrimination. If anyone chose hastily, impulsively, without careful consideration, he must not later on blame his fate on God.

The prophet now came down and placed the tablets on the ground so that everyone could have a preview and examine the life patterns at leisure before the lots were thrown. Er, who walked around with the others, was impressed with the great variety of lives available. There were, for instance, lives of power, of wealth, of fame; lives of virtue, of humble obscurity; lives of vice and carnal pleasure. But if one looked closely, reading the small print, so to speak, one would find that there were prices to pay for the tempting pleasurable lives. Great wealth, for example, might be followed with utter penury; years of unbridled sensual pleasure by years of terrible pain and suffering.

After sufficient time had been given, the prophet threw the lots, and each picked up the one that rolled nearest to him. Er noted that the lucky soul who got number one sprang forward eagerly, and chose the life of an absolute tyrant. When later he examined the details of the pattern more carefully, he found that, following the period of his absolute power and cruel tyranny, unspeakable evils would befall him. One was that he would be forced to eat his own children. Immediately he began to bewail his lot, blaming the gods, fate, anything but himself.

Another interesting point that Er observed was that the souls who had suffered long in Tartarus made, on the whole, the wisest choices, while many from heaven chose carelessly and foolishly. Suffering had brought some wisdom.

Other, and perhaps stronger, influences behind the selections were the former incarnations on earth. Old habits, hatreds, prejudices, special talents, ancient wrongs remembered, and so on, now seemed to play a big part in the selection of the next life pattern.

Ulysses, for instance, who was among the assembly, remembered the buffetings of his endless travels, the perilous adventures he went through, the emptiness of fame and the fickleness of fortune, and selected a life of quiet obscurity. He remarked that he would have made the same choice if lot number one had fallen to him.

After the selections had been made, and each now

knew the type of life before him, all proceeded to the Plain of Oblivion and "camped at eventide by the River of Forgetfulness (Lethe)." All drank water from this river, some more, some less, and thus forgetting all that had happened, they fell asleep.

Er was not permitted to drink the draught of forgetfulness and stayed awake to see the last act of the cosmic drama. After a time there was a tremendous noise, like a thunderclap, that awakened all the sleepers. Then some great power wafted them away in various directions. To Er they looked like shooting stars as they sped towards the waiting wombs of their next incarnations.

After that Er remembered nothing until he opened his eyes and found himself on his own funeral pyre.

All "beyond death" experiences have to be filtered through the waking consciousness in the remembering and the telling. They are, therefore, conditioned by the culture and understanding of the one who had the experience. In Er's story there are many symbols and mythological figures from his own ancient Greek culture. Yet, allowing for this, the story is basically compatible with the border-of-death experiences being collected today.

The Er story is, however, unique in that it includes a rebirth scenario. In my student days I could not accept the idea of reincarnation. Later I came to regard it as a reasonable, credible and, in a general way, quite acceptable doctrine. The odds are very much in its favor.

But whether one accepts the teaching of rebirth or not, some valuable philosophic truths are dramatized in the last scenes of the Plato story. These are, for instance, that our journey of life on earth comes from the lap of necessity, that chance plays only a small part in our lives; mostly, to paraphrase the poet, we are the masters of our fate; we are the captains of our souls. The story does not teach that all things are predestined. Only the patterns, the outlines, of our lives are ordained and we ourselves have selected those patterns. The details we fill in as we move along the broad road of our chosen destiny.

So it is wrong to blame fate, the stars or God for our sufferings and misfortunes for we ourselves are the authors of them. It is easier to understand and accept this truth in the framework of preexistence and former lives — lived either on earth or somewhere else.

The main objection that people have — and that I once had myself — to the idea of former lives is that we don't remember anything about them. The cutting off of all such memories is symbolized in the story by the Plain of Oblivion and the draught from the River of Forgetfulness. The Latin poet Virgil gives some reasons why we have to forget the past in order to live the new life to the best advantage.

Who from that draught reborn, no more shall know
Memory of past or dread of destined woe:
But all shall then the ancient pain forgive,
Forget their lives and will again to live.

The Mysteries

Socrates mentioned "the Mysteries" several times in his pre-death talk with his friends. But he did not say much about them. By their very nature the mystery religions of the ancient world were not an open book. The initiates were sworn to secrecy on pain of death, besides which they regarded the knowledge gained as sacred: pearls not to be cast before swine.

Inevitably, however, a certain amount of information leaked out in the course of time, and through comments in ancient writings combined with archaeological research, we can get a general, though not detailed, idea of what was taught about the meaning of life and death.

Esoteric religious centers existed in ancient Egypt, Greece and other countries. Herodotus, who was an initiate of the Mysteries, wrote: "On these matters, though accurately acquainted with the particulars of them, I must observe a discreet silence." Cicero praised the teachings but revealed no particulars either: "In the Mysteries we perceive the real principles of life and learn not only to live happily, but to die with fairer hope."

But some other writers gave a little more detail, and we can piece together part of what took place and discern some of the teachings given.

Eleusis near Athens was probably the largest and most famous of the centers. For over two thousand years people from all parts of the ancient world went there seeking initiation. The candidates included, not only leading philosophers and writers, but many Roman emperors. Yet worldly power was of no help to an applicant. Nero, for example, was rejected outright by the priests at Eleusis, and of all the imperial candidates only Hadrian passed the three degrees of initiation.

At Eleusis the rites, rituals and revelations were based on the Greek myth of Demeter and her daughter, Persephone. The story begins with a young maiden, Persephone, happily picking flowers in a sunny meadow of Attica (or Sicily, Arcadia or Crete — the setting varies). Suddenly the earth opened: King Hades appeared and carried her off to the Underworld in his black chariot.

Demeter, goddess of the fertile lands and corn fields, and generally regarded as the Earth-Mother, searched everywhere for her daughter, Persephone.

When at last she heard the truth of the abduction, she went to Zeus, the chief of the Olympian gods. Zeus was her brother and the father of Persephone. But, it seems, true to the Mafia morals of Olympus, he had done some dirty deal with Hades and was himself responsible for his own daughter's abduction. So he refused to help the sorrowing Demeter.

Then the Earth-Mother had recourse to the scorched earth strategy. On her orders all vegetation withered, and not a single crop was harvested for a whole year. If this was to continue, all life would soon vanish from the earth. Consternation and alarm gripped the Olympians. Zeus yielded. He sent a messenger, instructing Hades to return Persephone to her mother. Hades complied with the will of his chief, but cunningly, before sending his young wife back to the world above, he tempted her to eat seven seeds of a pomegranate from the orchard of the dead. This meant that Persephone would have to return to the Underworld.

Eventually a compromise was reached by which Persephone would spend nine months of each year with her mother and the other three months in the grey mists of the Underworld with King Hades.

It was at Eleusis that Demeter met and joyfully embraced her returning daughter. And there, before returning to Olympus, Demeter instructed some of her mortal friends, who had helped in the search, in the ritual of her worship. Thus the Mysteries began at Eleusis.

On the surface this appears to be a simple myth of the seasons. Winter comes and vegetation dies when Persephone goes down to Hades, and comes to joyous life again in the spring of her return. But to the esotericists it symbolized something deeper, and this deeper meaning was revealed in the Mysteries.

According to this deeper interpretation, the myth is an allegory of the fall of the soul into incarnation, its return for a period to the radiant world from which it came, and its periodic rebirth in the prison of the body and the dark world of physical matter. In the allegory, the sunny flowery fields where the child was first playing represents the soul's true spiritual home. Persephone symbolizes the human soul, and gloomy Hades represents the earth to which the soul, having once been there, must keep returning.

In the story Persephone could have stayed permanently in her true home if she had not eaten the seven seeds of the pomegranate. The incarnate human soul tastes the seven deadly sins of the earth, carnal desires are thus awakened, and these call the soul back to rebirth again and again.

Demeter represents the Divine Mother through whose great love the soul is able to escape temporarily its earthly bonds through death, and rise to the higher world. It is able to spend more time above than in the prison of the flesh. Thus the liturgical drama taught that death brings the soul's release from prison to a happier life. Yet while it is still tainted with earthly desire, it will return to earth. The memory of the flavor of the pomegranate seeds will call it back. Somehow that taste of earth must be expurgated, the emotional attachments, the longing for worldly pleasures must be erased before the soul's final release can be accomplished.

Two great philosophers of the ancient world — both initiates in the Mysteries — echo the idea that life on earth is really a form of death. Pythagoras said: "Whatever we see when awake is death." And Plato called the body "the sepulchre of the soul."

In the Mysteries there were apparently revelations in addition to the enactment and interpretation of the

Demeter drama. Some writers say that the goddess revealed to the spectators the glories and mysteries of man's future life.

Plato says in *Phaedrus*: "In consequence of this divine initiation, we become spectators of entire, simple, immovable and blessed visions, resident in a pure light."

Other initiates wrote of the visions in the divine light. Proclus says: "In all the initiations and mysteries, the gods exhibit many forms of themselves and appear in a variety of shapes, and sometimes, indeed, a formless light of themselves is held forth to the view; sometimes this light is according to the human form, and sometimes it proceeds into a different shape."

Thus the initiates seem to have been shown a great truth taught in the Hindu spiritual philosophy: the Divine can appear as pure, formless light (*jyoti*), but can also take on any form It chooses.

Some writers have said that the higher initiates of the Mysteries were taught that the Olympian gods had once been mortals on earth. The great lesson of this was that the soul of man can progress from the sufferings of earth, or the dreary life of Hades, to Olympian heights of happiness and the life abundant. This, too, I found later, is in line with the Hindu teaching in the *Yogavasishta*, that the gods of form and name (the higher as well as the lower) were once human beings. They had evolved through aeons of time to the high offices they now hold.

So, in my widening horizons, I found that from the simple mentality of the primitives to the great minds of ancient civilizations there had been a constant belief in life after death. Such pure belief, coming down from time immemorial, and accepted by men of the caliber of Plato and Pythagoras, must have come from knowledge and wisdom beyond reason. But I was in the iconoclastic age of reason. It was hard for me to accept anything on faith alone. In my search I needed empirical evidence, gathered by myself or by people whose integrity I could not possibly doubt.

If they hear not Moses and the prophets, neither will they be persuaded, though one rose from the dead.

Luke 16:31

3

Travellers Returning

Personal Investigations

With the label "agnostic" in my hat, I moved through the world and the years, ever alert for any sign of the evidence I sought. Though other things, many things, occupied the forefront of my mind, the search for the meaning of life and death was always there in the background — a theme song to which I listened in moments of silence. Such moments became less frequent, however, as the world moved through the uneasy thirties' into the forties' and the mad destruction of World War Two. But then the question of life after death waxed stronger in the public mind, and Spiritualism increased in popularity.

Death became a familiar figure to me on the battlefronts of the Middle East and Europe, but it remained as inscrutable as ever about the fate of the souls it harvested so plentifully. Did a rendezvous with a bullet mean a full stop to the comrade you had joked with at breakfast? Or had he gone on into some other dimension?

In Palestine, where I spent some months in 1942, I became friends with Lieutenant Bill Hand from a southern English county regiment. Bill was a handsome sporty type who occupied his leisure time in healthy pursuits like swimming and horse riding.

When one day, as we sat by a swimming pool, I asked him if he believed in life after death, I expected a disinterested, sceptical reply.

He answered without hestitation, "My father died when I was a child, and I have often heard his voice speaking to me. In fact, when I was young and out in the fields or woods of England, we would have long conversations together. Yes, of course I believe in life after death."

It seemed strange that Bill, "the body beautiful" as one brother officer called him, should be psychic and have no doubt whatever on the question that troubled me so much. Still, his answer pleased me.

Then later on, in the African desert with the Eighth Army, I got into a similar conversation with an American war correspondent named Hank Gorrell. He and I were spending a lonely Christmas together on the empty sands along the Gulf of Surti. In the evening, under the desert moon, we used to discuss all manner of things, and we became close friends.

Hank seemed a tough, swash-buckling fellow, proud of the fact that he had just flown with the RAF on a bombing raid over Naples. His bomber had been badly hit, and some of the crew killed or wounded. The plane had just managed to limp home to base in Africa. Hank was relieved and thankful to get back with his life and his feature story. After a few days in Alexandria, he returned to his regular assignment with the desert army.

But there was a Christmas lull over the battlefronts of the desert, so Hank and I celebrated the festive season with some plum pudding and a bottle of whiskey he had brought up from Egypt.

One evening, when the stars hung low, like lamps in an indigo sky, I ventured to bring up the question of life after death, and asked what he thought about it.

He took a sip of whiskey from his mug, looked up at the crescent moon over the sands, and began rather apologetically:

"Just a few nights ago I was lying in bed in the Hotel Cecil in Alexandria. In the middle of the night something woke me, and I was stunned to see my dead father standing by my bedside. The room was dark but he was sort of shining.

"My old dad had been dead for some years, you know. I thought I must be having hallucinations in the dark. So I switched on the bedside lamp. But I could still see him. Several times I switched the light on and off, trying to get rid of the apparition or whatever it was.

"Then my father spoke. 'I know you're testing to see if I'm really here, son. I'm here all right. I was with you in the plane over Naples too, protecting you from harm. Whatever happens, son, have no fear. I will always be protecting you.'

"It certainly was my father's voice, kind and deep, as it always used to be. He often called me son when he was alive, just as he did now. And as he went on talking — on personal matters — there were other typical mannerisms of speech that made me sure it was really my father.

"Funny, too, the room got very cold as if the phantom of my father had lowered the temperature. I found myself shivering. That, with my nervousness and tension, made me smoke cigarette after cigarette.

"I don't know how long he stayed, but finally, he just seemed to fade out before my eyes. I put my head under the blankets and tried to sleep, but I was still shaking with the cold and shock.

"The first thing I saw next morning was the ashtray on my bedside table, loaded with butts and half-smoked cigarettes. I knew for sure then that the harrowing experience had been real. Also I caught a cold from the freezing atmosphere my dad had somehow brought in with him. I'm still sniffling, as you no doubt have observed.

"If you had asked me the question previously, I might have said that belief in life after death was probably superstition or wishful thinking. But now I know that death is not the end. My father was certainly very much alive the other night in my room at the Hotel Cecil."

The stories of these two friends who, like Hamlet, had seen or heard their fathers' ghosts, brings me to an experience at my own father's death in Sydney, Australia, a couple of years before the war.

He and I had always been good companions. When I was a boy we had camped and hunted together in the Tasmanian bush, and fished its sparkling streams. Though his formal education had not gone beyond the primary school, his alert mind had reached to higher levels. I found I could discuss with him my thoughts from the widening horizons of student days, and he always had something worthwhile to contribute.

When he knew that he had a disease that was probably incurable, he began to read the Bible daily. Perhaps he could hear the rumble of Pluto's chariot wheels drawing closer. But he was only sixty-five, and it seemed to me quite impossible that the chief cornerstone of my world should be torn away. Some time he had to go, of course, like everyone else, but not now, surely!

Then he was put into hospital and given new treatment under a new doctor.

When I visited him there one evening, he seemed to be on the mend. My hopes for his recovery soared high. Death retreated over the hill.

Next morning, as I stepped from my apartment into the brilliant spring sunshine, the sky went suddenly black from horizon to horizon. At the same time an unbearable depression engulfed me. I stood trembling under its impact, while shapes that seemed like ravens of ill omen came out of the gloomy sky and swooped towards me.

Then, as suddenly as it had come, this black psychic veil was swept aside, leaving the baby blue spring sky and dazzling sunshine. The experience was quite inexplicable to me as I hurried to the station and caught my train to the city.

I had scarcely sat down at my office desk in a building near Wynyard Station, when my telephone rang and a voice told me that my father had died. In fact his death had occurred that morning at about the time I stepped into the vision of blackness and depression. I felt then that it had been a death sign to me and also, in a way, a precognition of the deep gloom I now began to feel.

Precognition being the only psychic faculty that had ever manifested so far in my life, I felt little hope of any communication from my father, even if he was still in existence — a matter on which I was by no means certain. My only hope of any such thing lay in my psychic mother. So, about a week after my father's funeral, I asked her if she had had any signs of him.

"Yes, I felt his presence here for several days after his death. He seems to have gone now, though."

Eighteen years later, after I had been through the war and travelled the world, learning something of life and death, but not their deepest secret, I was sitting beside my mother's deathbed.

For nearly a year she had been bed-ridden. During my visits to her, we had talked at times about life after death. I found that she had at last abandoned the dogma of the sleep of the soul and the resurrection of the body. She had no doubt about a hereafter, though, and felt sure she would at death be re-united with my father and all the loved ones who had gone on before.

But I myself did not want to think about her approaching end; and did not encourage her to talk about it. In fact, I kept assuring her that she would recover and walk again.

I did not really believe it, however, and know now that I should have faced the truth with her, allowing her to say whatever she needed to say at this critical time.

But, the idea of walking again did appeal to her, and she pretended to believe my words — perhaps for my sake, for I think she knew the end was near. Another thing that had worried her during the last years was her failing eyesight. She often remarked that her eyes were dim, and she had a great longing for clear vision. These two salient desires of her last months, to walk again and to see well, play an important role in my later experience.

The night she died I was holding her hand. I did not think that she was actually about to leave me till I heard the death rattle in her throat, and she was gone. But there was no dramatic vision, no psychic experience, as I had more than half expected at the death of one who certainly had the "second sight." Simply, one moment she was there and the next she was gone. It was inexplicable that an event of such shattering importance to me could happen thus, while the mundane world rumbled on unconcernedly.

After we had laid her ashes to rest beside my father's in a wall at a Sydney crematorium, I knew that the time had come for me to make a renewed onslaught on the defenses of the undiscovered country. I joined the Psychic Research Society of Sydney, and began attending meetings with mediums and clairvoyants.

The medium held in the highest regard by the officials of the Society was an ordained minister of the Church of England. He was known as a direct voice medium, which meant that voices would be heard coming through a trumpet some distance from the medium while he was in a trance. I decided to go to his regular weekly meetings held in a house in a southern suburb.

On my first visit I found that the meetings were held in a large room specially set aside for this purpose in a garden. The people attending — perhaps about thirty of them — sat with their backs to the wall, forming a rough oval. Before starting the séance, the medium made the sign of the Cross on two trumpets. I noticed that these instruments, the shape of megaphones and made of some lightweight metal, had phosphorescent marks on them. This meant that they would reveal their location in the dark.

"Does the medium wear a luminous sign on his jacket?" I asked the official of the Society who organized the meetings. "Or do you tie him to his chair?"

"No," he replied, "we have tested him thoroughly and are quite convinced of his honesty."

Fine for you, I thought, but what about new observers like me? This is more like an ordinary Spiritualist séance than a psychic research meeting.

"I must ask you not to strike a light in the dark after the medium goes into a trance. It could do him great harm," said the same official.

I had heard that this was so, and promised to

refrain from such tests.

The trumpets were placed in the middle of the room on the floor. The medium took off his shoes, sat in his easy chair and relaxed. All the lights were put off, leaving the room in complete blackness, and there were sounds of heavy breathing from the medium as he, presumably, went into his trance.

Soon voices began coming through the trumpets which could be seen floating about in the dark, like two fireflies. Sometimes a trumpet would soar up to the ceiling. At times there were two voices, one from each trumpet, both holding a discussion with any sitter who cared to join in. One discussion, on the subject of reincarnation, developed into a debate between the two trumpets. One believed in it and the other — claiming to be a deceased priest — did not.

The voices that came through during the evening were of different types, quality and tone, yet all, whether male or female, held a trace of the voice of the medium. This aroused my suspicion at the time. But in later studies I found that this is so in genuine phenomena because, it is said, the communicators take ectoplasm from the vocal organs of the medium to construct the etheric "voice box" they use for speaking into the trumpet.

Sometimes a trumpet went around tapping people on the head, a common gimmick at Spiritualist meetings. As in this place our chairs were backed against the walls, in order to do this tapping himself, the medium would have had to move around close in front of us — a risky performance as some sitters might have their legs stretched out in front of them.

I went to a number of meetings with the minister-medium, hoping for some word from my mother. Generally speaking, the messages from the communicators were on a higher level than those I had experienced at any Spiritualist séance I had attended before, but were still rather mundane and trivial, I thought. If they proved life after death, they also proved that the level of intelligence there was even lower than on this side of the grave.

Moreover, I was not absolutely convinced that the whole thing was genuine. One evening, a voice claiming to be that of the father of a young German in attendance came through a trumpet and made a few remarks to his son. A superficial dialogue ensued, and the son did not sound satisfied. Then he spoke to his "father" in German. There was no reply.

"I would like to converse with you in German," the son said in English.

"We speak nothing but English over here," the voice replied sternly, and went "off the air."

This shattered the last remnants of my faith and, as I had no sign from my mother, I decided to save the weekly ten shillings that the meetings were costing me.

About a year after my mother's death I went to see a clairvoyant named Anne Novak, who was on a visit to Sydney, and giving private readings in her room. My fiancé had made the appointment and, to the best of my knowledge, the clairvoyant knew only my name and nothing more about me.

I came into her room as a stranger, and when I did so, she said, "Your mother has just walked through the door with you." She gave a brief description of my mother, and then proceeded to relay messages from whatever entity was present with us in the room.

One was: "Your mother says to tell you that she can now walk again, and that her eyes are not so dim."

This statement was certainly spot on the two things that had been worrying her before her death. But why, I wondered, should she *walk* in the astral when she could presumably float or fly. Also, surely her sight would be perfect now, not simply less dim than during her last years on earth!

There was another message that puzzled me somewhat, too. She echoed some advice that she had often given me before she died, which was to renew a broken link with a woman who had gone abroad. My mother did not seem to know the current situation; she had evidently not perceived the fact that I was engaged to a woman she had never met. Soon afterwards I married this woman, and the union brought me the companionship and contentment that my mother had always wanted for me.

But why now, as I stood before Anne Novak with my heart full of love for my fiancée, did the message say I should travel abroad and repair a broken romance with someone I had found untrustworthy? It certainly seemed to show that neither the clairvoyant, nor whoever might be communicating through her, were able to read my mind or see into my heart.

Another message gave a possible clue to the mystery. It was: "Your mother asks why you always go around in a cloud of thought."

I feel that I do put a cloud of concentrated thought around myself, often abstract thought. This might well create a barrier making telepathic rapport difficult. It is well known that communication with another dimension of existence is easier when there are no obscuring clouds of intellectual mentation around one.

Another message that seemed strange, but became clearer in the light of further study, was: "Tell him that his efforts to reach me since my passing have been a great help to me."

Later study in psychic fields threw some light on the puzzling points in the messages. I learned, for instance, that the newly dead do usually walk until they learn to float or glide or fly. Even then they sometimes walk.

Regarding her sight, there is evidence to show that physical disabilities sometimes remain in the astral body for a time and vanish only slowly. It is all a matter of the mind. When the discarnate person can think positively that the astral body is perfect in health, it will be perfect. This can take a little time, but not as long as it takes to "think" the physical body into health and harmony in this world.

The fact that I had been trying so hard to make contact with her was a proof of my love for her, and constituted a kind of prayer for her welfare. There is much spiritual and psychic revelation to support the view that love and prayer for the departed are a great help to them.

A study of many spiritist communications have shown that, as a general rule, the souls of the dead are not able to see our physical bodies or physical objects, except in the presence of a mediumistic person. Many of them can see our auras and peer into our minds to some extent. But not all can read all minds, and mine may have been, as my mother indicated, a difficult mind to penetrate.

Was it really my deceased mother communicating? I have thought about this question a good deal in the years since that meeting with Anne Novak. The alternatives are: one, that it was a part of the medium's subconscious mind digging into my mind; or two, it was one of those impersonating entities from the invisible world who love to communicate with this one, playing any appropriate role.

If it was either of these, they did a poor job of mind reading — and the low spirit pretenders, in particular, are supposed to be experts at mind probing, and also to be rather clever at reading the future.

On the whole I am inclined to think it was, in fact, my mother. Anne Novak was just the type of person with whom my mother would have had rapport, and whose aura might well have attracted her. This medium, I think, provided the right conditions for her to communicate and satisfy my great desire to find her still in some extra-physical existence.

After that event I tried no more to make contact, as I did not want to hold her back near the earth.

The Society for Psychical Research

A few years later my wife and I were sojourning in London, and there I joined the British Society for Psychical Research (S.P.R.). My reason for this was twofold. I was still trying to penetrate the undiscovered country, and I had a journalistic project in hand. I had been asked by a London magazine to do a series of articles on parapsychological subjects. The S. P. R. provided some of the material for the articles.

Founded in 1882, the British Society for Psychical Research was the first organization to attempt to examine in a scientific spirit and manner those fringe phenomena called psychic and parapsychological.

The Society was conducted by people of high academic or scientific standing, and it tried to carry out its investigations in a purely rational manner, without prejudice.

While they labored hard to probe the unexplained powers of the mind, the matter that seemed to have occupied members most in the early days was the question of life after death. This is understandable for several reasons. The upsurge of physical science, and particularly the theories of Charles Darwin, were routing the old theological beliefs about life and death.

Man was not, after all, it seemed to many of the intellectuals, made by God in His own image, as stated in Genesis. Instead, man had evolved through immense periods of time from the animal kingdom. He was not a soul from the divine breath, but a body with the evolutionary trimming called consciousness. It was logical, if sad, to conclude from this that at death man would return to dust. As an individual he would cease to be.

It was perhaps in reaction to this bleak picture of man's destiny that a few intellectuals, Cambridge dons and several leading scientists, set out to test the truth of this new concept. They would, they decided, test it by the very methods that had brought it into being — the objective observation, controlled experimentation and cold, impersonal reasoning of physical science.

Among the leaders of this new venture were some of the outstanding men and women of the day. They included, for instance, the famous psychologist William James, the philosopher Henri Bergson, scientists Sir William Barrett, Sir Oliver Lodge and Lord Raleigh, J. J. Thompson, who discovered the electron, the great biologist, Alfred Russell Wallace, who propounded the theory of evolution at the same time and independently of Charles Darwin. The group also included Lord Balfour and Sir William Crookes, considered the greatest scientist of his time.

No doubt another factor concerned in the birth of the S.P.R. was modern Spiritualism. This, starting in America in about 1848, had spread in three decades throughout the western world. Thousands of people were claiming that their dead were speaking to them through mediums in the fashionable drawing rooms of all the great cities from New York to St. Petersburg. Serious investigators asked themselves if this was true or if the people were being fooled by clever mediums, or perhaps deceived by some unknown powers of the mind.

For their investigations the S.P.R. used both professional and non-professional mediums. But first they tested them thoroughly for integrity as well as ability. A number of mediums passed the stringent tests. Some of them, like the famous Mrs. Lenore Piper of America, were employed by the S.P.R. investigators for many years.

A great deal of material was amassed, both through mediumistic communications and in other ways. In appraising the material the S.P.R. took a stance that they considered completely unbiased, unaffected by the former popular theological beliefs or by deep-laid emotions. They followed, they claimed, the Law of Parsimony. This meant that hypotheses, or explanatory theories, should not be multiplied needlessly in attempting to explain phenomena.

The way this stance seemed to work out in practice was that messages must not be regarded as coming from deceased persons if they could be explained in any other way. Explanations always more acceptable than the survival hypothesis were: telepathy between living people and clairvoyance by living people.

Such explanations were often taken to great lengths. If the information received through a medium, when in trance, existed in the medium's subconscious mind or in the mind, conscious or subconscious, of any one of the sitters present, it must be assumed that the message might have come from such a mental storehouse. This was preferred to the assumption that the dead survived.

Furthermore, rather than postulate the soul's survival, it was considered more scientific to assume that a medium could probe the mind and memory of any person anywhere — even if miles away, even if quite unaware that the relevant information was buried in his subconscious mind. He may, for instance, have picked up the facts subconsciously, and never been consciously aware of them. Yet the distant medium could dig them up from his mind.

Even though no such tremendous telepathic powers of the human mind had been proved, the investigators preferred to postulate their existence rather than accept the simple explanation that the dead were communicating. Was this, one wonders, in keeping with the Law of Parsimony? While striving not to be biased in favor of age old and emotionally charged beliefs, were they not perhaps prejudiced *against* those beliefs in their attempt to be coldly scientific?

Because almost all the information coming through mediums existed in the mind of someone living somewhere, and could presumably be tapped by the omniscient mind of the medium, it seemed impossible to establish proof of life after death by this method. Occasionally, however, facts not held in any living person's mind did come through from another dimension.

There was, for instance, the famous Chaffin Will Case. James L. Chaffin, a farmer from North Carolina, U.S.A., had four sons. When he died in September, 1921, a will was found, duly attested by two witnesses, and dated November 16, 1905. According to this he left his property to his third son, leaving nothing to his widow and other three sons.

Four years later, in June 1925, the second son dreamed a vivid dream in which his deceased father stood by his bedside. There were several such dreams before the father managed to say: "You will find my will in my overcoat pocket." Then the apparition vanished.

When the old overcoat was finally located, a piece of paper was discovered, stitched to an inside pocket. On the paper was written: "Read the 27th chapter of Genesis in my Daddy's old Bible." The dusty old Bible was opened at the appropriate place, and a will, dated January 16, 1919, found there. This will ultimately received probate, making all four sons heirs to their father's property.

To common sense this appears to be a case of a father returning to put right an unjust situation. Why he took four years to do this we don't know; it may have something to do with his condition after death and the difficulty of communicating. Several of the S. P. R. investigators did regard this case, and several similar ones, as evidence of the soul's survival of death.

Others, however, preferred alternative explanations. In the Chaffin Will Case, for instance, some investigators said that the son who had had the dream might have observed the existence and location of the will by clairvoyant means. Then his dream consciousness had staged the dreams to bring the information through to his conscious mind, and spur him on to action.

But surely this is a forced explanation. The dreams would scarcely have been necessary to bring such clairvoyant perception to the conscious mind of the son, and induce him to take action on something liable to benefit him financially. Moreover, this explanation assumed the existence of clairvoyance which had not been scientifically proved to the satisfaction of most S.P.R. members. Was it then more scientific to postulate clairvoyance rather than the survival of the dead? Some seem to have thought so.

Voices that speak regularly through a medium, and claim to be souls of the departed, have been called "familiar spirits" and "spirit guides." The S.P.R. investigators called them "controls" and assumed that they were personalities emerging temporarily from the unconscious depths of the medium's mind.

If a century of work by the S.P.R. has not proved scientifically and absolutely the reality of life after death — and few members would say that it has — it has, alternatively, proved some fantastic powers of the human mind. In themselves these powers are strong evidence that man is much more than the materialistic image of him: just a body with some trimming called mind emerging from it.

It must have seemed to the honest investigators laboring in the last decades of the nineteenth century that when all phenomena could be explained by the extrasensory powers of the mind, demonstrable test-tube proof of the soul's survival was really impossible.

Then with the turn of the century came a strange gleam of light and hope. Frederick W. H. Myers, one of the Cambridge dons, a classical scholar and poet, who helped pioneer the S.P.R., passed away into the unknown land. This was in 1901 and soon afterwards he appeared to be communicating, but in a new and special way.

The communications seemed to be a planned attempt to circumvent the stumbling block of telepathy — as if from one who understood the basic problem. Part of a message, incomprehensible in itself, would be given through one medium, perhaps Mrs. Piper, then several more fragments through other mediums, such as Mrs. Holland in India and

Mrs. A. W. Verrall in England.

When from some clue given through one of the mediums the pieces were put together, the message made sense. Furthermore, it would carry the characteristic stamp of the sender, Myers. That is, it would probably be about some obscure subject in classical mythology or history that Myers would have known.

Apart from the fact that the messages came piecemeal through several mediums, none of the mediums concerned had the very specialized knowledge conveyed, nor in many cases would such knowledge be accessible from the mind of a living person.

The series of messages were given the name "cross-correspondences." The eminent psychologist Professor Gardner Murphy has defined a cross-correspondence as "a series of fragmentary phrases or sentences, each essentially without significance, but which, when put together, give a clear message."

Frederick Myers was soon joined by other communicators — all recently deceased S.P.R. investigators, well known while alive. Two of them were, for example, Professor Henry Sidgewick of Cambridge and Edmund Gurney, both philosophers and scholars. The number of communicators increased as S.P.R. investigators themselves passed into the undiscovered country. The cross-correspondences went on for three decades.

The mass of material acquired was still being studied and assessed by members of the S. P. R. when I visited their offices in Adam and Eve Mews, London, during the 1960's. From the three thousand odd scripts received through mediums over thirty years, there was a great deal of work to be done in fitting the pieces of the literary jigsaw puzzles together.

Reports of cases are too long to give a detailed

account of any of them here. The case known as the 'Ear of Dionysius' (the name of a grotto in Sicily) takes, for instance, forty typed pages to give in full. The fragments, coming through two different non-professional automatic writers, dealt with obscure classical subjects beyond the education of the mediums concerned.

A heterogenous mixture of fragments was received in this case, as in most others, and there seemed for a long time to be no common link between them. The communicators seemed to be two recently deceased friends of Frederick Myers, both university professors of the classics while alive.

Finally they provided clues that led the investigators to a little known American textbook entitled *Greek Meltic Poets* which was collecting dust on the bookshelves of one of the deceased communicators. In this book was an account of a minor Greek poet named Philoxenus of Cythera. Only a few lines remain of the work of this obscure classical poet. And in the textbook found among the communicator's books was the only known account of Philoxenus in a form containing all the references given in the scripts of this cross-correspondence. It seemed to be a valiantly planned attempt by two deceased classical scholars to prove their identity and continued existence.

Only a small proportion of the texts have so far been published, and they fill volumes. But have the Herculean efforts of communicators and investigators finally proved that the dead survive? For some of the S.P.R. researchers, yes; for others, no.

Eleanor Sidgewick, widow of Henry Sidgewick, an ultra-cautious woman of science, said of the cross-correspondences: "I, myself, think that the evidence is pointing towards the conclusion that our fellow

workers are still working with us." Her brother, Lord
Balfour, said that, after much study and reflection,
he "leaned strongly in favor of an affirmative
answer." To S.P.R. member J. E. Piddington, a practical businessman who had spent a good part of his
life on the scripts, the evidence therein brought conviction of the fact of life after death. Professor C. D.
Broad said that the evidence made it hard to resist
the conviction that the mind of a person survives the
death of his body and continues to think and plan.

Such statements are typical of a proportion of the
members who thought that the soul's survival had
been proved to reasonable minds by this empirical
evidence. But others were still not convinced that
such proof had been established. They argued that
the mediums concerned might be in telepathic rapport, sharing relevant information with one another.
Of course, as well as sharing little known facts, they
would have to agree on a plan for giving out the
information in disjointed fragments that would
finally fit together. This would be quite a feat in
unconscious telepathic communication for mediums,
some of whom did not even know each other, and
lived in different parts of the world. "Scientific" bias
against the continued existence of the soul affronts
common sense in such far fetched explanations.

Some researchers thought that the whole astral
plane experiment to prove the soul's survival, if such
the cross-correspondences were, was poorly exe-
cuted. The British parapsychologist, Dr. Robert
Thouless, put it this way: "If this was an experiment
devised . . . on the other side of the grave, I think it
must be judged to be a badly designed experiment.
It has provided a mass of material of which it is very
difficult to judge the evidential value, and about
which there are varying opinions . . . A successful

experiment should give a more clear and unambiguous answer to the question it is designed to answer than does spontaneous material; otherwise the experiment is not worthwhile."

So after the cross-correspondences, as before, the S.P.R. researchers were divided into those who accepted survival (the survivalists) and those who did not (the anti-survivalists) — with perhaps a higher proportion of survivalists than before. The debate still goes on.

It seems to me that a century of hard work has failed to provide the proof of survival that the S.P.R. members require. For one thing, the job has been handicapped by the paradigm of nineteenth century science: the false assumption that nothing exists beyond the material. Whereas twentieth century science has advanced to the point where non-material facts can no longer be excluded; in fact, to the point where physical matter itself is seen to have no existence beyond the mind.

For another thing, the researchers have been asking for the repeatable, mathematically demonstrable type of proof that cannot be obtained with the kind of materials in which they deal.

Establishing the reality of man's survival of death is more like a case in court than an experiment in the laboratory. In court the evidence is usually circumstantial, and even when there are eyewitnesses, doubt can be thrown on their veracity or reliability as observers. A verdict must be reached by the judge or jury on the weight of evidence one way or the other. The truth is never a mathematical certainty.

Judging empirical circumstantial evidence on life after death should follow the same model. If the evidence is strong enough to convince a majority of reasonable, unbiased minds, the verdict should be given accordingly. There will always be dissenters from the verdict. Even science, pausing to prove each step of the way, has never made a big step forward without dissent.

Along somewhat similar lines of thought, the humanist Colin Brookes-Smith stated in an S.P.R. journal that the evidence from cross-correspondences, favorable to the fact of man's survival of death, cannot *all* be brushed aside, for alternative explanations are less credible than the spiritist one.

Survival, he claimed, should now be regarded as a sufficiently well established fact to be beyond denial by any reasonable argument. This conclusion, he states, should not be kept in the obscurity of research records, but should be presented to the public "as a momentous scientific conclusion of prime importance to mankind that must ultimately lead to a radical alteration of human outlook throughout the world."

Another S.P.R. investigator, who agrees that survival has been proved beyond reasonable doubt, suggests that psychic research in the future should not be concerned with the fact of survival, but with the question of "the exact meaning of such survival."

Many of the S.P.R. investigators themselves realize there is a big gap between what they know and that which they can definitely prove by their prescribed methodology. One of their eminent researchers and writers once said to me, "We have not *proved* life after death, but I know personally from my own experience that such a life exists."

Sir William Crookes

Born in 1832, William Crookes was married at the age of twenty-four and elected Fellow of the Royal Society when he was only thirty-one. A year afterwards he was made joint editor of the prestigious quarterly *The Journal of Science* and later became its sole editor. He was a leading light in the world of science throughout his life.

A dormant interest in the perennial problem of life after death is, in many people, triggered into action by the loss of someone close and dear. William Crookes seems to have been one of these. His younger brother, Philip, to whom he was greatly attached, died at the age of twenty-one, and the same year a man called Cromwell Varley interested William in methods of "communication with the dead."

At the age of thirty-seven, some thirteen years before the foundation of the Society for Psychical Research, William Crookes began the serious, systematic study of psychic phenomena.

In a letter written soon after he began these investigations, he said, "Historical testimony is overwhelming as to the fact of communications having been made to mortals from invisible intelligent beings distinct from the human race: and contemporary evidence to similar occurrences is accumulating daily."

He went on to say that the subject could be approached from its theological side or examined in its scientific aspect, but, "I am likely to do most good by following the bent of my own intellect, and examining the subject purely in its scientific relations." In such an investigation the scientist should, he said, suppress all romantic and superstitious ideas, and "be guided by hard intellect alone."

As his wife, Ellen, was also interested in the research, Crookes was able to carry on his observations and experiments in his own home in London, where conditions could be kept firmly under his control. Meetings were held there frequently (about twice a week) and went on for many years. Crookes employed some of the most outstanding mediums of the last century, including the famous D. D. Home.

Like other investigators of the time, he was able to observe on many occasions, and under conditions controlled to his scientific satisfaction, the amazing physical phenomena of levitation, powerful apports, the passage of matter through matter, materializations — even to the materialization of the full human body — and many examples of lesser physical phenomena.

Crookes kept his psychic investigations as exoteric as his other scientific work and reported openly on his findings in *The Journal of Science.* The reactions of his intellectual colleagues were mixed. Some, like Sir Oliver Lodge, were themselves interested in this line of research. A few, like Francis Galton, he was able to draw into his séances. But the greater sceptics, who knew and admired Crookes as a scientist, were completely bewildered. They knew not what to think. "I cannot disbelieve Mr. Crookes's statements, nor can I believe in his results," wrote Charles Darwin, typically.

Henry Sidgewick, in 1874, some years before he helped to found the S.P.R., quoted a friend as saying, "There are only three alternatives — Crookes is either affirming a tissue of lies, or he is a monomaniac, or the phenomena are true." But the hardline sceptics were strongly against his spiritist activities. Some laughed, while some attacked him venomously.

Thomas Huxley expressed the correct scientific attitude to new phenomena when he said, "Sit down before a fact like a little child, be prepared to give up every preconceived notion, follow humbly to wherever and to whatever abysses nature leads or you shall learn nothing." But he failed to measure up to his own standards when the newly formed London Dialectical Society asked him to join them in an investigation of spiritist phenomena. Prejudice, intellectual pride, or whatever it was, overcame his worthy dictum, and he replied that he was no more interested in their offer than he would be to listen to the chatter of old women and curates in a distant cathedral town. This expressed the general attitude of the so-called scientists of the day.

But undeterred by opposition and ridicule, William Crookes carried on, probing like a true scientist into the facts of psychic phenomena, heedless of what it might do to his reputation. His high status as a scientist, however, withstood the attacks of his critics as shown by the honors showered upon him.

In 1875 he was awarded the Royal Medal by the Royal Society. Later he was knighted and made President of the British Association. Later still, despite some forty years dabbling with the spooks, he was awarded the Order of Merit and made President of the Royal Society.

These honors were signposts of his great achievements in the search for truth in nature. But how was he faring in his search for truth in supernature? Though he stated that for him this search must be according to the guidelines of science, in the style of the S.P.R., he did not ignore the resurgence of a different approach to the mysteries.

In 1883 William Crookes became a member of the Theosophical Society which had been founded in 1875 to explore the great unknown through other avenues and by other methods. He remained a member for the rest of his life.

Mr. C. C. Massey, a London barrister who was an early member of the Theosophical Society, wrote in a letter to Colonel Olcott, its President: "I sat next to William Crookes at dinner the other night and had a very interesting conversation with him. Indeed, neither of us spoke a word to anyone else all the time. He is an Occultist, and a pupil of Eliphas Levi, whom he met in Paris. . . . He is going to write to you, being interested in finding the similarity of results at which you have both arrived."

But Crookes' main thrust was along the scientific path and, though this proved to him the reality of occult forces, it brought continued disappointment in establishing proof of man's survival of death. In 1874 he wrote to a woman in St. Petersburg who had asked the great scientist if he had found such a proof:

"To 'fix the identity of a deceased person' has been the chief object I have had before me for the last three or four years, and I have neglected no opportunity myself on that point. I have had almost unlimited opportunities of investigation, more so perhaps than any other man in Europe. Mr. Home has scarcely given a séance in England during his recent visits without my presence at it, and most of his séances have been at my house or at my brother's.

"In addition I have had frequent séances with all other good mediums whose names are familiar to Spiritualists.

"During this whole time I have most earnestly desired to get the one proof you seek — the proof that the dead can return and communicate. I have never once had satisfactory proof that this is the case. I have had hundreds of communications *professing* to come from deceased friends, but whenever I try to get proof that they are really the individuals they profess to be, they break down. Not one has been able to answer the necessary questions to prove identity; and the great problem of the future is to me as impenetrable a mystery as ever it was. All I am satisfied of is that there exist invisible intelligent beings who *profess* to be spirits of deceased people, but the proofs that I require I have never yet had; although I am willing to admit that many of my friends declare that they have actually received the desired proofs, I myself have been very close to conviction several times."

In his kind-hearted way, Crookes finishes the letter with these words: "I am extremely sorry that I can give you no more comforting assurances. I have passed through the same frame of mind myself, and I know how earnestly the soul craves for one little sign of life beyond the grave."

Crookes did not come lightly or easily to a conclusion. That there were communications from an invisible world he had proved beyond doubt by 1874. But after another forty years of continued psychic research, he had not come to the definite conclusion that the communicating entities were spirits of the dead.

In May, 1916, his wife died. Sir William was much stricken by the loss and, no doubt, longed more than ever to obtain unimpeachable proof of life after death. Yet, towards the end of the same year, Sir Oliver Lodge wrote in a letter to the editor of *Light*: "I never feel quite sure how far he [Crookes] is satisfied with the evidence for survival itself. He inclines to it very strongly no doubt; but ancient scientific scepticism takes a good deal of weakening before it gives way, and is liable to recrudesce at times in a surprising manner.

"In a note to me he says that he rather envies me the absolute proof I have obtained about the continued existence of my son. I gather that he rather wishes that he could obtain similar absolute conviction about the continued existence of his wife, with whom he lived for over sixty years. But this is not a matter to touch upon in print."

Shortly afterwards Sir William Crookes obtained, at Crewe, with a medium named Mr. Hope, a piece of evidence that gave him the final proof he needed. It came in the form of a spirit photograph of his late wife.

In the course of two letters to Sir Oliver Lodge during December, 1916, Crookes, who was an expert photographer himself, made these statements about the spirit photograph.

"I went into the question of photographic trickery many years ago and from the confessions and admissions I had from tricksters, I am acquainted with all the dodges possible. In my case at Crewe, the plate never left my possession except for the minute when Mr. Hope put it in and took it out of the camera. He could not possibly have done anything to deceive me. I did all the manipulating and developing myself. The picture I developed on the plate is not a facsimile of any photograph ever taken of my wife.

"I am glad to say the possession of this definite proof of survival has done my heart much good."

During the following year Crookes had communications with his wife in a series of remarkable materialization séances at his own home at 7 Kensington Park Gardens in London.

Crookes was a member of the S.P.R. and another member, Miss F. R. Scatcherd, gives an account of one of these séances in a book entitled *Survival* (Putnam, 1924).

Apart from Sir William, she states, there were only Mrs. Z., the medium and herself at the séance. The lights had been put out and the phenomena had started when someone outside the room opened the door. It was afternoon and a shaft of light fell on the medium who gave a gasp of agony. Miss Scatcherd called out, "Shut the door. You are spoiling our experiment."

The door was shut, but not properly, and a bar of light shone through. In this, Miss Scatcherd saw a bulky shadow pass between Sir William and herself. Thinking that this meant the medium had left her chair, she stretched out her hand to see if this were so, and hit the knee of the entranced medium who was sitting rigid in her chair.

At the same time Miss Scatcherd heard a voice say, "You have hurt my medium. She was already suffering on account of the light." The voice, presumably that of the spirit control, went on to say that they (the unseen forces) were shielding the medium from the bar of light, and that there was no need to close the séance.

Miss Scatcherd was able to see what looked like ectoplasm arranged in such a way that it sheltered the medium from the light. She could also hear a lively conversation going on between Sir William and the spirit of his wife. Crookes was sitting with his back to the door, and was not assisted by the bar of light. He told his wife that, though he could feel the touch of her hand, he was sorry that he could not see her.

She replied, "I am here beside you, Willie dear. Listen while I carry the music box around the room."

Miss Scatcherd then saw the ectoplasm form into a gripping apparatus.

"By means of the bar of light I saw the music box as it was whirled past the door and round and round Sir William's head. . . . It was passed gently up and down his injured leg (he had suffered a fall). And most of the time two or more voices were speaking with Sir William and myself. . . .

"I had known Lady Crookes during her lifetime, and was now witness of her attempts to make use of ectoplasm as a means of demonstrating her survival, by actions and effects that needed only the register of the normal five senses for their perception.

"The medium was ill for some time as a result of the shock caused by the sudden letting in of the light. Also, where I had placed my hand on her knee in order to ascertain whether she had left her chair, was a huge dark bruise which only gradually disappeared during the next few days, and was at first painful to the touch."

But though all such evidence was no doubt very comforting to the eminent scientist, it seems to have been the Crewe photograph that brought conviction. It showed his wife, he said, about ten years younger than when she had died. There had been no photograph of her taken at that period and there were none in existence like the "spirit photograph." This could not, therefore, have been duplicated from another photograph, even if there had been an opportunity for the medium to do so — which there was not.

So, working for years along the guidelines of science, one great scientist obtained the proof he needed and died at the age of ninety-seven believing that there was a life beyond the grave.

But he would not have claimed that his long labors in this field had established scientific proof for everyone. The experiments that convinced him are not repeatable at will by other investigators. Rather than take the word of one man, many would say that, great man and scientist though he was, he could have been deceived or been hallucinating.

Yet this question is of such prime importance that what we need to do is to open the door towards truth for the science oriented mind of mankind today. And so the tireless research goes on, with new men and women trying new methods.

The gods conceal from the living how pleasant death is, so that they will continue to live.

Lucan, *Pharsalia*

4
From the Borders — New Approaches

Deathbed Visions

Moving away from controversial communications through mediums, the spearhead of psychic research is taking new directions. One of these is the scientific study of deathbed observations made by doctors and nurses. Another is the collection and analysis of reports from people who have been declared dead, and were, in fact, clinically dead. But, like Plato's Er, they returned to tell their tales. A third new source of comparative evidence is the memory regression of individuals under hypnosis. In such regressions there are sometimes memories of earlier lives and earlier deaths.

Not long ago I came into personal association with the two leading exponents of research on deathbed visions. These are Dr. Karlis Osis, then Director of Research at the American Society for Psychical Research (ASPR), and Dr. Erlendur Haraldsson of the Department of Psychology at the University of Iceland, but previously a research assistant at the ASPR.

During the 1960's, while a member of the British SPR, I had read Karl Osis' excellent booklet, *Deathbed Observations by Physicians and Nurses*. He called this a pilot study in the field. It was a survey of cases in America. Later, when the full report of a cross-cultural survey embracing both America and India was completed by the two researchers, Dr. Haraldsson kindly sent me a copy of it.

How many thousands of deathbed visions have gone unrecorded through the centuries? One only has to bring up the subject among people to hear some spontaneous accounts.

Only the other day, a woman, named Carin, told me about her father who had been in hospital for an operation. He was recovering quite well, but his doctor thought he should take a sea cruise to help him regain his strength. His family arranged for the cruise and bought the necessary tickets. A few days before he was to be discharged from the hospital, Carin (the daughter) was sitting with him in the ward.

Suddenly he looked up towards the ceiling, and a beautiful smile of joy broke over his face. "Mother!" he cried, and dropped back dead. His mother had been dead for several years. The man himself was certainly not expecting to die; he was, in fact, looking forward to his cruise.

Another friend, named Lyn, told me that when her mother was nearing death she was sitting by the bed, holding her hand. She loved her mother dearly, and did not want her to go.

The mother closed her eyes and was silent for some minutes; then she opened them and said: "Rita just came to take me, but you would not let me go." Rita, who had been dead some years, was the mother's greatest friend. It was as if a strong love had called her to the other side, but a stronger one had held her back, temporarily.

Reports of deathbed visions are current in most families. A dying person may, like Carin's father, speak to someone who is invisible to everyone else in the room. He may say, like Lyn's mother, that the invisible visitor has come to take him to the next world, or he may not. Often such visions change the dying person's mood from gloom, or apathetic resignation, to happiness or overwhelming joy.

The sceptics say that such visions are only the hallucinations of a sick and delirious mind. Spiritual people, on the other hand, take them at their face value, as signs of loving care either by good friends who have gone before, or by some kind of angelic guide or helper.

If these visions are actual, if there is, in fact, something there, and they are not just mental delusions, they offer interesting evidence for life after death. This does indeed seem a promising field for the searchlight of scientific study.

The first to see the possibility, and to do something about it, was Sir William Barrett, then Professor of Physics at the Royal College of Science in Dublin. He was also one of the early members of the SPR in Britain. Sir William collected a number of deathbed observations made by physicians and nurses, early in this century, and noted a few striking features.

For instance, the dying person would at times be surprised to see, with the apparition of the dead at his bedside, the figure of a friend he thought to be still alive. He would exclaim about this. But the fact was that the "living" friend had recently died. Neither the patient nor others in the room had heard about this death.

Such experiences, thought the researcher, were strong indications that apparitions at a deathbed are not just products of the dying patient's expectation. He may expect to see perhaps a beloved friend, or the figure of Jesus, if he was a devout Christian, but he would not expect to see someone he thought to be still in the land of the living.

Another striking feature noted by Sir William was that dying children, who had been taught that angels had wings, and seen pictures of them with wings, would sometimes exclaim with great amazement that an angel *without* wings was present by the bedside. This suggested a reality rather than a mental delusion.

Sir William Barrett's interesting findings, published in 1926 in a little book called *Deathbed Visions*, inspired Osis and Haraldsson to do more comprehensive research along these lines.

In America, after the pilot study by Osis, the two researchers sent out questionnaires wherever appropriate. Practically all the physicians and nurses who were given questionnaires filled them out and returned them to the researchers. This was then followed up by personal interviews.

Some idea of the amount of work and time involved in this research will be gathered from the fact that a total number of 877 cases, about evenly divided between America and India, were studied by the two men. Then a computer was used to classify and evaluate the mass of material gathered.

The survey showed that the most common type of bedside vision by dying patients was the seeing of people who had died before them, though great religious figures, such as Christ and other forms of God, were also frequently seen. Sometimes heavenly abodes and beautiful landscapes came into the dying vision.

Bedside visions were usually of short duration, five minutes or less. Some, however, the survey showed, lasted up to fifteen minutes, and a few went on for an hour or more.

In both America and India the dying patients stated generally that the phantom visitors had come for the purpose of taking them away. The greatest proportion of patients consented eagerly to go with their visitors. The elation and serenity brought about by such visions contrasted strongly with the customary gloom of the death chamber.

Some of the patients, however, did not consent to go, and a few reacted with terror, and screams for help. For some reason, unknown to the investigators, practically all the patients who reacted violently against being taken away were Indian.

This may, perhaps, have something to do with the fact that Yama, in *Vedic* times a benign lord of a pleasant home beyond death, has become, in modern Indian culture, a terrible lord of vengeance. If such a figure came into a deathbed vision, the patient would naturally react with fear and resistance.

The survey showed that the Indian patients predominantly saw religious figures — not always Yama — whereas American patients generally saw human beings they knew to be dead. Naturally, the religious figures appearing to each national group varied according to the two cultures — Jesus or Mary, perhaps, for the Christians, and Shiva, Rama, Krishna, Durga, Yama or some other form for the Hindus. Usually, however, the religious figure was not identified, being described simply as an angel or a god.

But in appraising these visions there are certain questions that the researcher must ask and attempt to answer. One is that, as not only dying people, but others have hallucinations and visions of various kinds, why should those seen at the hour of death be any indication of a life beyond death? An answer lies in an analysis of the two types. Visions seen by people who are not nearing death are predominantly of living folk, according to research on the subject. In other words, they see the astral body of someone still alive, though possibly residing a long way off. The purpose of the visitation, stated or telepathically understood, usually has nothing to do with the imminent death of the recipient.

On the other hand, in deathbed visions the apparitions are mostly of someone known to be on the other side of death, and the visit is intimately connected with the death of the recipient, most often to help in the transition.

Another important question is: are the visions simply hallucinations resulting from the dying patient's belief in a life after death? The research shows that such deathbed visions come to those who do not believe in a hereafter, as well as to those who do. Osis and Haraldsson state: "Our analysis revealed that a belief in an after-life has no significant influence on the frequency of the kind of apparition seen." In fact, the occurrence of deathbed visions of a world beyond death seems to be quite independent of any belief or expectation.

Of course, drugs are often given to the dying, who are, moreover, frequently in a state of stress. These factors are known to induce or foster hallucinations. So a pertinent question is: could any of them be the cause of visions reported by dying patients?

Our two researchers give the answer to this in their report: "The majority of patients about whom we have such information had not received drugs which could cause hallucinations." And about the possible effects of stress, they conclude from a close analysis of the material: "While the stress experienced by the terminal patients might have caused other kinds of hallucinations, it is unlikely that it affected the incidence of apparitions which expressed purposes related to *post mortem* survival."

Visions at the hour of death appear to be very real things, but a riddle is this: why do some people experience them while others do not, or at least do not report them to anyone present? There are examples of both classes in my own experience. My Aunt Harriett, for instance, heard heavenly music and saw visions of deceased loved ones just before she died. My mother, on the contrary, saw nothing, for if she had had any experience, I feel sure she would have mentioned it to me at the time. Both women were equally religious, with firm belief in life after death; both died slowly after long illnesses.

Psychic research in other directions indicates that at ordinary slow deaths there is nearly always a helper who, knowing, comes from the other side to give assistance in the transition. The helper's timing may not be exact, however; he may arrive before the dying patient loses consciousness or after. If a vision of otherworldly figures, or sounds, or landscapes, comes after, even a moment after, the consciousness of this world has faded out, the patient will obviously not be able to report it.

This is a possible explanation of the riddle, but there may be others.

Researches along slightly different lines tie up with, and amplify, the evidence gleaned from death-bed visions.

There and Back Again

There are a good many people who, like Er, have gone to the border, or just beyond the border, of death and kept their return tickets. They have had glimpses, and sometimes more than glimpses, of the undiscovered country. They have placed one foot across the line that divides the afterdeath world from this one.

Of course, we would not say that a traveller knew Germany just because he had changed planes at Munich Airport or Egypt because he had viewed its shores from the Suez Canal. But he would, at least, be sure that such places existed, and have some impressions to relate. If the impressions from a number of independent travellers had common features, we would not say that the travellers had been dreaming.

As medical resuscitation techniques are improving, more and more people are being brought back from beyond the border of clinical death. These are people who have died in the sense that medical science cannot detect any life in them. But, either through persistent scientific resuscitation, or some other agency, they have returned to life. This surely offers a good, and widening, field for research on the soul's survival.

Pioneers in the field are not parapsychologists or professional psychic researchers, but two medical doctors: the internationally renowned lecturer, psychiatrist and writer, Dr. Elisabeth Kübler-Ross, and Dr. Raymond Moody Jr., who has written best-sellers on the evidence he has collected for the truth of life after life, as he calls it.

Both doctors, working independently and then unknown to each other, reached similar insights and conclusions. Dr. Kübler-Ross has stated her conclusions clearly and courageously before audiences of her sceptical, materialistic colleagues of the medical profession. They are that, through her work in thanatology, from both deathbed visions and the experiences of the near-dead, she *knows* there is a life after death and, moreover, has no doubt whatever about the truth of reincarnation. She has done a tremendous job in turning the tide of public opinion away from the horror of death to an understanding interest in it. She has taught people how to die happily. She has taught doctors and nurses how to help their patients towards, and through, the great transition.

Dr. Raymond Moody has stated that, although he is quite aware that his evidence does not constitute a conclusive proof to the scientist, he himself feels sure that there is a life following the end of this one. So many people who have died clinically, and been declared or presumed dead by their doctors, have come back and told him about their experiences on the borders of the life to come.

Though not all the travellers have had precisely the same experiences, there are important features of the immediate beyond that have been perceived by a great many of those who made the return trip. From these common perceptions, experiences and impressions a general statement can be made about what has happened, after clinical death, to many people.

First there is a noise like a buzzing or ringing of distant bells, or something similar; then the patient seems to go through a dark place, like a tunnel or cave or deep valley. Both these experiences probably arise from the passage of the astral body from the physical body.

Then the patient realizes, often with great surprise, that he is not his physical body. He sees the latter lying on the bed, or perhaps the operating table. He observes what the doctors and nurses are doing and hears their conversation. He tries to speak to them but they neither hear nor see him. Or it may be that he tries to comfort his bereaved family, but neither are they aware of his astral presence. Yet he seems to have a body just like the one lying inert on the bed.

About this time he may experience dual conscious-

ness, seeing, as well as the people around his dead
body, entities from another dimension. While the former ignore him, the latter see him and speak to him.
They may be friends or relatives who have died earlier, or perhaps some other kind of spiritual helper.
These beings bring comfort, answer questions puzzling his mind, and tell him that everything will be
all right. Usually they seem to know that the patient
is not irreversibly dead, but not always. They may
tell him that his time has not come, but sometimes
the patient feels that the helper is there to guide him
across the border.

Many of those who returned to tell their stories had
encountered a great spiritual entity whom they called
the Being of Light. The radiance of the light was itself
the most striking thing. None saw an actual figure
within the light, yet they felt the presence of a great,
warm, loving personality there. They felt a deep love
and understanding that flowed from the light and
enfolded them. Some tried to identify the personality
within the radiance as Christ or a great angel. Others
did not. Both religious and non-religious people contacted this Being of Light, and it was the most beautiful thing in their *post mortem* experience.

Shortly after its appearance the Being begins to
communicate with the patient. This appears to be a
direct telepathic communication and seems to take
the form of a question, such as, "Are you ready to
die?" or, "Are you satisfied with what you have done
with your life?"

The questions are never asked with condemnation
or accusation, however, but with total love and
understanding. The purpose of the questioning
seems to be to make the patient examine his own life,
and to help him towards a true understanding of
life's purpose.

Then comes a moment of tremendous intensity when the person concerned sees a panoramic review of his life. This is not like ordinary remembering. It is so rapid that everything seems to appear at once. The whole life can be seen and reviewed in an instant of earth time. Yet it is incredibly vivid, in color and three-dimensional.

Some people even felt again the emotions they had gone through at the time each event took place, and some also felt the emotions of other people concerned in the events. In one sense it was like watching a movie, yet the watcher was playing the leading role. While watching himself and feeling himself re-live his life, the person was able to pass judgement on it from a higher perspective.

So in a way this review was like the particular judgement of some religious teachings, but the soul was passing judgement on itself. The great Being, standing aside, was simply giving the person the opportunity to judge himself. But through this self-judgement he was able to learn some valuable lessons from the errors of his past years. The two most important of these were: one, that we must learn to love everybody; and two, we should continue to acquire knowledge right up to the end, for learning is a continuous process that goes on after death.

The glimpse of after-death life, beings and heavenly scenes are so joyous, so elevating to the mind that most of those who have had the experience do not want to return to their physical bodies.

However, they are made to understand that they must go back. Then some have the sensation of being drawn down through the dark tunnel up which they had gone. After that they lapse into unconsciousness and awake to the pain and sufferings of the body. Some startle and puzzle their doctors or relatives by telling them what they were doing and saying near the body they had thought was an unconscious corpse.

People who have been through such an experience have no doubt whatever about its reality and importance. It has, they say, quite a different quality from hallucination. The brush with death and visions beyond change their lives profoundly. They get life and death in a new perspective. They become open to new knowledge and want to start learning again. Hearts previously closed become open to God's love, and this flows out to their fellow men. Many traditional dogmas about the hereafter vanish, as does the materialist's dogma that there is none. Perhaps most significant of all, the person who has "died" is no longer afraid of death.

Among the people who have "died" and come back to life was my old friend Walter Cowan of Orange County, California. He went through some of the experiences outlined above, but not all.

Walter was a man who, by the time I knew him, was in his seventies, and had achieved considerable success in both worlds. He was a self-made millionaire and he had made some good strides along the path towards spiritual enlightenment. By various routes he had come eventually to Sri Satya Sai Baba.

During the Christmas period of 1971, Walter and his wife, Elsie, were in Madras, India, staying at a well known hotel there. They were in Madras because Sai Baba himself was on a visit there.

John Hislop, another American businessman and seeker after the spiritual, was also in Madras, and a witness to some of the strange events that took place that Christmas. He recorded an account of them on tape, and this was later printed in a number of journals. Below are some highlights from the Hislop account.

"Early Christmas morning, news spread among devotees gathered about Sai Baba that an elderly American had suffered a fatal heart attack. Upon hearing the rumor, my wife and I at once went to the Cowans' hotel where Elsie confirmed that her husband had died.

"Walter's body was taken to the hospital by ambulance.

"At my request Judge Damodar Row of Madras interviewed the doctor who had attended Walter when he had arrived at the hospital. The doctor's statement was that Walter was indeed dead when he examined him, shortly after the ambulance had arrived at the hospital. There was no sign of life. He pronounced Walter dead. The body was covered with a sheet and moved into an empty room.

"Later that day when Elsie and her friend, Mrs. Ratanlal, went to the hospital, they found that Sai Baba had already been there. To their utter amazement they found Walter alive.

"Sai Baba informed his devotees that he had indeed brought Walter back to life."

When Walter Cowan was sufficiently strong to be moved to Bangalore, where Sai Baba had gone, Dr. Ganeswaran was his attending physician. John Hislop, who had known this doctor for years, says: "He had obtained Walter's medical history with its specific laboratory tests showing severe diabetes of long standing, and various other diseased conditions." The doctor now made some laboratory tests of his own and found that the symptoms of diabetes and the other diseases had completely vanished.

Later, Walter's private secretary in California said that, after his resurrection from the "dead," his mind was "twenty years younger." So, for some mysterious reason, his experience while clinically dead had removed his chronic bodily diseases and rejuvenated his mind.

About his experiences on the other side of death Walter said: "I found myself very calm, in a state of wonderful bliss; and the Lord Sai Baba was by my side. There was no anxiety or fear, but a tremendous sense of well-being.

"Then Baba took me to a very large hall where there were hundreds of people milling around. This was the hall where the records of all my previous lives were kept. Baba and I stood before the Court of Justice. The person in charge, who knew Baba well, asked for records of all my lives. He was very kind, and I had the feeling that whatever was decided would be the best for my soul.

"The records were brought into the hall: armloads of scrolls. As they were read, Baba interpreted them for me. In the beginning they told of countries that had not existed for thousands of years. . . . But when they reached the time of King David, the reading of my lives became more exciting.

"As the reading continued, it seemed that what really counted were my motives and character. . . . As I incarnated in the different countries, I carried out my mission — which was for peace and spirituality.

"After about two hours, they finished reading the scrolls, and the Lord Sai Baba said that I had not completed the work that I was born to do, and asked the judge that I be turned over to him to complete my mission of spreading the truth. He requested that my soul be returned to my body, under his grace. The judge said, 'So be it.'

"The case was dismissed and I left with Baba to return to my body. I hesitated to leave this wonderful bliss. I looked at my body and thought that it would be like stepping into a cesspool to return to it, but I knew that it was best to complete my mission so that I could eventually merge with the Lord Sai Baba. So I stepped back into my body ... and that instant it started all over again: trying to get my breath, being as sick as you could be, and still be alive."

After hearing this account, John Hislop asked Satya Sai Baba if it was some sort of hallucination or real. Baba replied that it had been a real experience. Asked if every person has a similar experience at death, Sai Baba said, "It is not necessarily so; some may have similar experiences, some not."

In the main features Walter Cowan's experience was similar to those of many of Dr. Moody's subjects who went through clinical death. Cowan saw his physical body lying on the bed. He felt a great peace, well-being and a wonderful bliss. He was met by a spiritual Helper, his own *paramaguru*, Satya Sai Baba, who, though still alive on earth, travels at will in a subtle body on any plane of existence. He was guided by this Helper into a scene beyond death, aided in his experiences there, and then led back to his body.

The "review," however, had several facets that were different from the typical model of the researchers. Scenes were not brought before the eye like a movie, but read out from scrolls. Many lives were reviewed, which was in keeping with Walter's cultural background and understanding; his spiritual search, much of it in the Hindu teachings, had brought him to a complete acceptance of the truth of reincarnation.

Like most of the people in the researches on this type of experience, Walter was very reluctant to return to his body.

Before this experience, he had been able to travel consciously out-of-the-body so, as a result, he did not have much of the usual fear of death. But after the clinical death experience he had no fear at all.

Following a further eighteen months of happy, healthy life, doing whatever it was he still had to do on earth, Walter finally died, easily and peacefully, at his home on Cowan Heights, Orange County, at the age of eighty-two.

From the Living who Died Long Ago

Some aspects of the death scenario, drawn from deathbed visions and after-death experiences, are supported from quite another approach — from the memories of those who went through death long ago and are now back living on earth. At least, this seems to be the situation from hypnotic regression into memories of former lives. Also, there are a few who somehow skipped the Lethe draught and remember past lives and deaths without the aid of hypnosis.

The purpose of deep memory regressions, carried out by research workers, is often to test the evidence for past lives and the truth of reincarnation. They do, however, at the same time bring out occasional vivid memories of past deaths.

In recent years, a number of researchers have been working in this field, and several have received a good deal of publicity.

Helen Wambach Ph.D., an experimenter in the San Francisco Bay area of California, reported in *Psychic* magazine (Nov/Dec 1976) on her researches into nearly a thousand past lives. About the death aspect of these she writes: "During hypnosis I took participants to the death experience in past lives to see if their descriptions matched those of people who had clinically died and been brought back to life. I did give the option to subjects to avoid the death experience if they were frightened of it, and about twenty per cent of my subjects did skip this experience."

The eighty per cent who were quite prepared to go through the old death memory revealed some interesting things. The majority of them had had natural deaths from illness, many in old age. Others were from accidents, violent deaths in war or skirmishes, and a good percentage from childbirth. These latter were remembered as being difficult and sad deaths. But deaths in war and other violent situations were not usually experienced as more traumatic or difficult than natural deaths.

"In fact, often a feeling of relief and pleasure occurred immediately after a bloody death in battle. One subject was blown up by an artillery shell in World War One. I asked him to look down on his body, and he answered: 'There is no body — it is all blown away. Oh, very pleasant this dying — I see now it was all a game.'

"Perhaps the most pleasant deaths were those from old age: 'I'm not really ill. I'm leaving my body because it's time. I've done all I should have and I'm tired.'

"Sixty-three per cent of my subjects expressed relief and calm acceptance just before death and just after the spirit left the body. Another twenty-three per cent felt transcendent joy at death, and described it as a marvellous feeling of soaring away into freedom: 'The body lying there looks so small. I'm glad I'm not confined to it anymore,' was a common way of expressing this feeling. Sometimes the emotion was: 'That was a dull confining life. I'm glad I don't have to endure those limitations anymore.'

"Only twelve per cent of my sample felt fear, sorrow or regret during the death experience. Most of these were women dying of childbirth or those who felt they had left things undone.

"The most amazing statistic to me was that, even though a sizeable minority of my subjects had no belief system regarding life after death, only three per cent were surprised that they survived death. This could mean many things, but to me it means that nearly all of us, at a subconscious level, believe that we survive death."

Scenes from lives going back into prehistoric times were recalled, the majority being the simple lives of peasants. Death was remembered among these as an accepted, undisturbing part of life. "The transition seems natural and easy; it's time to go, and I die." Many made remarks to this effect as memories of their primitive lives came back to them.

An astounding case of one who recalled a past life and a terrible death, without the aid of hypnotic regression, was a woman patient of the British psychiatrist, Dr. Arthur Guirdham. He met the woman first when she came to him about her persistent nightmares. He was then chief psychiatrist at the Bath Hospital, England.

Her apparent memories of a life in the south of France in the thirteenth century were so amazing that Dr. Guirdham travelled to the relevant area himself to investigate the evidence. His study of old manuscripts — available only to scholars with special permission — showed that his patient was accurate in every detail in her descriptions of thirteenth century people, places and events. In the archives he even found some of the songs she had, as a child in this life, written out in medieval French.

The woman had been a Cathar, a heretical group in Toulouse, at the time of her former life. Her knowledge of their practices, the lay-out of buildings, the family and social relationships of people, not found in the history books, but traced in the records of the

Cathar Inquisition, were accurate. Guirdham was helped in his historical investigations by French professors who were specialists on the period. The evidence left him no alternative, he said, but to accept reincarnation.

His patient remembered the massacre of the Cathars, and her own death at the stake in terrible detail. This traumatic death had been the cause of her recurrent nightmares. It had also, probably, exploded a breach in her wall of forgetfulness and brought to life her other old memories.

She had earlier written down the nightmare about her death in shorthand and transcribed it for Dr. Guirdham. In it she describes the maddening pain, the utter agony that makes her forget to pray to God; the surprise when she finds herself bleeding heavily in the blazing heat; the hope that her blood, hissing in the flames, will put them out. The worst part, she says, is her terror of the fingers of flames reaching to pluck out her eyes; she tries to close her eyes but cannot: her eyelids seem to have been burned off.

But her greatest surprise is when she suddenly turns icy cold, numb and cold. She begins to laugh. She has fooled the people who tried to burn her. "I am a witch," she thought, "I have turned the fire to ice." Some of the aspects highlighted in these studies of dying and dead patients, and other fields, are confirmed or explained by the work of another investigator.

Dr. Robert Crookall held an important position in the Geological Survey of Great Britain before he retired early to devote himself to psychic research. His method was to examine all the evidence from both Spiritualism and psychic research. A great mass of such material had, of course, been accumulated since mediumistic communication began about 1850, and researchers brought their scientific methodology to bear on it thirty years later. Crookall looked for internal consistencies within the evidence, whether it came from popular or research literature. If a salient feature appeared again and again in evidence from different sources, he took it to be significant, and probably a true experience.

In a summary dealing with the fate of the average person at death, he makes some interesting points in the light of the results from the other studies. He states that a person dying a natural death (as opposed to a sudden accidental or enforced death) knows sub-consciously that he is about to die and sends out telepathically a "call" to the beyond. The person about to die is not consciously aware of taking this mental action. But it is this "call" that brings some-one, usually a loved one, or perhaps a great spiritual helper, from the other side at the hour of death.

Those who die suddenly are not able to send out this telepathic "call," and consequently the help from the spirit world is mostly delayed. This delay may be short or long, and in the meantime the soul is often bewildered, not knowing that death has actually taken place.

On other relevant points, Crookall states that the ethereal double arising from the physical body at death is made up of both the astral (soul) body and the etheric vehicle. It is the severing of the "silver cord," attaching the double to the physical body, that causes final and irrevocable death. Until this hap-pens, the soul can be recalled to the apparently dead body. The cord may be broken immediately, or not for some days, after clinical death, but usually not more than three days.

While the cord is still intact there is dual vision; the dying person can see both the sensuous and the supersensuous worlds — alternately, or at the same time.

There is usually a brief coma at the time of actual passing, as the consciousness leaves the body and is not yet established in the astral body. This may be the period that patients experience as travelling through a dark tunnel, cave or valley.

A short review of the past life comes at about this time, often following the coma. But the longer judgement takes place later, after the etheric vehicle has been shed. This shedding Crookall calls the second death. Then the Higher Self reviews and judges the life lived by the personality. The Gallery of Memory is entered and pictures of the past life pass before the person concerned. He re-lives the emotions and thoughts, not only his own, but of other people involved in the events. He sees all his errors, all his sins.

Mercifully, he also sees his little acts of kindness and compassion, his selfless efforts to help his fellow men. These may be few, but they are a tonic to a weary soul, filled with remorse for its many mistakes, its lack of love and understanding.

This sounds very like the "review" experienced by the clinically dead in the presence of the Being of Light. The latter may be the resplendent, shining Higher Self, the *Manasa Taijasvi* (radiant Higher Mind). It is the true Self of the soul with whom it will eventually be united.

However, there is a point that needs some clarification here. When a clinically dead person experiences the review, he can scarcely have shed his etheric vehicle and gone through the "second death." The first death must be completed before this takes place. Yet, according to Crookall, the soul cannot experience this review while the etheric vehicle is still attached to it.

One can only conjecture, therefore, that in the case of a near-death experience of the review, the etheric vehicle has remained temporarily attached to the physical body. This can happen as it is merely a bridge between the two bodies. The astral can move alone out of the physical, leaving the etheric bridge still enmeshed with the physical body. Then the astral would be free to go through its wonderful experience of meeting the Being of Light who supervises the self-judgement.

This, or something like this, as Socrates would say, may be the truth of the matter.

We will try to follow, in subsequent chapters, the soul's far from simple journey into the depths of the undiscovered country, from the borderlands to the great heights.

I have been in that heaven the most illumined
By Light from Him, and seen things which to utter
He who returns hath neither skill nor knowledge;
For as it nears the object of its yearning,
Our intellect is overwhelmed so deeply
It never can retrace the path it followed.
But whatsoever of the holy kingdom
Was in the power of memory to treasure
Will be my theme until the song is ended.

Dante: The Divine Comedy

5

From Those Who Went to See

Mainly Theosophical

A casual suggestion by a member of the Theosophical Society in London was to lead to a deepening of my search for death's meaning. It was that we should stop in India on our way back to Australia, to which we were returning after four years in Europe. In India, the member said, we should attend the School of the Wisdom which was conducted annually at the International Headquarters of the Theosophical Society at Adyar in Madras.

As we had been members of the Society for several years, and wanted to improve our understanding of Theosophical concepts, we decided to do this. The course of study, we were informed, lasted six months, from October to the end of March, and it dealt with aspects of the Ancient Wisdom on which Theosophy is based. So, in the latter half of 1964, we sailed by Dutch cargo ship from Genoa, in Italy, to India.

The Director of Studies for the School that year was the late I. K. Taimni, a doctor of science, a Theosophist and an occultist in the best sense of that term. The Principal of the School was the late N. Sri Ram, President of the Society, and a fine open-minded, philosophical lecturer. Other outstanding lecturers were the English seer Geoffrey Hodson and the leading American Theosophist James Perkins.

The Ancient Wisdom is like a mighty banyan tree with its central trunk in India, and its widespread branches rooted in most countries throughout the world, to form the bases of the great religions. After studying its central roots, we planned to wander through India, getting to know the sacred soil that had nourished this great tree of knowledge. This plan we carried out.

But, as our subject is the meaning of death, we must confine ourselves to that facet of the Wisdom.

Several of the *mahatmas* of the great White Lodge of Adepts, who were the behind-the-scenes founders of the Theosophical movement in the last century, had some things to say on this facet. Their observations can be read in their published letters to A. P. Sinnett.

Then the second generation of Theosophical leaders, particularly Bishop C. W. Leadbeater and Dr. Annie Besant, had a good deal more to say. What they said has been summarized by Lieutenant-Colonel Arthur E. Powell.

Concerning their method of investigation, Powell writes: "The most skilled of the Theosophical investigators are able to transfer their consciousness at will to the astral plane, or even the mental (heaven) plane, and bring back to the physical brain the recollection of experiences. In this manner has been derived a large proportion of Theosophical knowledge."

So their method, in contrast to that of psychic research, was to travel to the invisible worlds in spirit or supernormal consciousness, and report what they had discovered about the soul's journey beyond the doorway of death.

At first Annie Besant and C. W. Leadbeater collaborated in this work, but in 1912, five years after she became President of the Society, Besant left most of the psychic investigations to Leadbeater.

Charles Webster Leadbeater was a remarkable Britisher. He started life in an unremarkable manner by becoming a clergyman in the Church of England. But in the 1880's he met that outstanding occultist, Madame H. P. Blavatsky, while she was on a visit to England. This meeting seemed to open up some deep wells of knowledge, perception and yearning in the English curate. Soon afterwards he came into contact with one of the founding *mahatmas*, and the upshot was that he left the Church and went with Madame Blavatsky to India.

To begin with, his main work was in the Society's new educational program for Buddhists. Then he became Annie Besant's chief helper, and spent much of his time on clairvoyant investigations, lecturing and writing. He also later on helped establish the Liberal Catholic Church and became one of its first bishops. Like most remarkable public personalities, particularly those with occult powers, C. W. Leadbeater became a controversial figure, and is so still.

Leadbeater gives a more detailed account of the undiscovered country, and life there, than any other seer or occult group — or, at least, any with which I am acquainted.

Of course, we cannot, with our five senses, check the observations of these flyers to the supersensuous worlds. So, if we are to consider their reports at all, we must accept them, for the time being, on faith or through an intuition of truth. Then we can compare the different "travellers' tales" with each other, and with the teachings of the religions, and be in a better position to judge their intrinsic value.

The Theosophical investigators confirm the Wisdom teachings that the world awaiting man beyond death can be divided into two main spheres. Various names may be found for these in occult literature, but we will keep to the Theosophical terminology, calling them the astral and mental planes.

In one sense, the planes and their various subdivisions may be called states of consciousness. It is known from common experience that, as our state of consciousness alters, so does the environment we see around us. In dreams, for instance, we see a different world from that of our waking state. Again, when our consciousness alters under the influence of certain drugs, such as LSD, an entirely different world comes into existence for us. The dream world, the drug world, the world of the trance state, and so on, seem to the perceiver at the time quite as real as does the physical world to the waking consciousness.

Are any of them actually real? Science has shown that matter is nothing more than energy moving in certain patterns at certain rates of vibration. The whole physical world, therefore, does not exist as such; it is a mental concept projected onto the energy patterns that affect our human senses in certain ways.

Death brings a major change of consciousness and this projects another world — seeming quite as real as the one we have left behind. It is in fact as real, and as unreal. This is the astral plane and, like the physical plane, it is mentally created by the influence of new patterns of energy (known as astral matter) on the subtle senses. Both, like all phenomenal worlds, have a verisimilitude of reality. But true Reality lies beyond them.

The astral and mental planes do not belong to our three-dimensional space. They do not exist somewhere out beyond the sky, but here where we are. The only journey we need to make to reach them is a journey in consciousness. And that is the journey that the clairvoyant investigators make. A certain change in consciousness will bring anyone into the subtle inner worlds.

Theosophy divides the astral planes into seven sub-planes. The lowest of these has the physical world as its background, though only a partial and distorted view of the latter. It is a dark, depressing, gloomy place, like the classical Hades. Four thousand years ago the Egyptian scribe Ani paid this sub-plane a visit and wrote on his papyrus, "It is deep, unfathomable; it is black as the blackest night, and men wander helplessly about therein; in it a man may not live in quietness of heart."

Climbing up the ladder from this depressing darkness, we find the next few sub-planes very similar to the earth but becoming more luminous; and higher still we come into the radiant worlds that justify the epithet 'astral' (shining) which is given to the whole plane.

In the mid-zone of the astral are the regions that play a large part in popular religions and mythology. Valhalla, the Happy Hunting Ground, Elysium, Summerland, the various Paradises, and such, exist here.

Beyond the highest sub-plane of the astral is the mental plane, also known in Theosophy as the heaven plane, or Devachan. This, likewise, is divided into seven sub-planes, each becoming more celestial and spiritual as we rise higher. The three topmost sub-planes of the mental are also known as the causal plane, or the highest heavens.

The main purpose of going through the astral plane seems to be purification. There are important lessons to be learned, the dross of selfishness and low desires must be purged away before the soul can journey onward to the heaven world. All souls must travel through all the sub-planes of the astral. But only the lowest types — violent criminals, drunkards, drug addicts, and the like — would dwell for any length of time in the lowest zones.

Ordinary decent folk would pass through this terrible area swiftly, and perhaps unconsciously, awaking to find themselves on one of the higher sub-planes. But if their lives have been selfish, pleasure seeking, trivial, worldly, they will have to spend a long time on one of the intermediate sub-planes.

On the two highest sub-planes of the astral are to be found the unspiritual religionists and the intellectual materialists. Many may be happy to remain there for years, doing no good to anyone, and making but little progress on the upward spiritual journey. Indeed, they are often sceptical of the existence of anything higher than the place where they are.

Time spent on the astral plane varies a great deal according to the individual's former life and spiritual development. Some rare souls may pass through in a few minutes, going straight on to heaven, as it were. At the other end of the scale, there are some individuals who spend many years, even centuries, there. The average person, according to Leadbeater, can be expected to remain in the astral for about thirty or forty earth years. But how long this may seem to the astral dweller is another matter, for time is psychological there more than here.

Straight after death the appearance of the astral

body is practically the same as the physical body. It remains similar to the human earthly form throughout, but there are some changes. The astral dweller can decide, for instance, whether he wants to appear young, middle-aged or old. Most who die when old return to their looks at the prime of life, but Sri Yukteswar Giri, the great *guru* of Yogananda, elected to keep the appearance of old age.

Another point is that the astral body reveals the inner character much more truly than the physical body does. So, as a soul becomes more spiritual, the face and form reflect its spiritual beauty. On the other hand, the denizens of the lowest sub-plane soon take on a bestial appearance in keeping with their characters.

The gifted clairvoyant Edgar Cayce, writing of journeys upward through the sub-planes of the astral, said that, after seeing his body lying motionless below him, he felt trapped in an oppressive darkness. Then he became aware of a beam of light and struggled upward towards it.

"While I am ascending the path of light," he said, "I become ever more conscious that I am passing through different levels on which there is a great deal of commotion. On the lowest level I see vague but frightful shapes, grotesque forms like those seen in nightmares. Then on all sides monsters begin to appear, parts of whose bodies are incongruously large."

He went through more changes of scene and mood until he reached his goal: the place and people with whom he felt a spiritual affinity.

Those who take hallucenogenic drugs also often experience the ugly, bestial forms and menacing atmosphere of the lower astral before they reach the higher happier levels.

For a time after death the average person will continue, through mental habit, to do some of the things he did on earth. He may continue to walk, to eat meals, to drink cups of tea, and so on. But eventually he finds that life is different. By the power of thought he can fly from one place to another, or even travel instantaneously, at the speed of thought. He does not need to eat, but will do so while he feels the desire. He does not need to work in order to live; everything he requires is created when he wants it by the mental force that molds the astral matter.

Some, who have worked too hard on earth, may take a long vacation like the overworked housewife who wrote for her epitaph: "Don't mourn for me now; don't mourn for me never; I'm going to do nothing for ever and ever. "

But many astral dwellers continue to work at things they enjoy doing, or perhaps things they felt frustrated about not being able to do on earth. Thus clairvoyant visitors find them engrossed in all kinds of occupations, such as writing, composing music, painting, teaching newcomers to the zone, also nursing the newcomers who imagine themselves to be still sick. Through the joy of creative and selfless work, they help their own spiritual progress there, just as people do here.

But all is not sweetness and light for everyone all the time. There are the hells for those who need them. Clairvoyant investigators have not found the imaginative traditional hells, the seven-walled, down under, dark region of the Babylonians, the Japanese hell, Jigoku, with its eight regions of fire and eight of ice, nor the Greek Tartarus, nor even the Christian lake of fire and brimstone. But hells there are, nevertheless. The astral sub-plane near the earth sounds very like one. And Leadbeater talks, in hushed tones, of something even lower. This, which he calls the Eighth Sphere, is a place of destruction. It is for a person who has lived an extremely degraded life, without one gleam of unselfish thought or feeling to light it. His immortal Higher Self has decided that he is beyond redemption, and has withdrawn, leaving a soulless personality. It is this empty façade, this simulacrum that goes to the Eighth Sphere, "there slowly to disintegrate after experiences best left undescribed," writes Leadbeater.

The Mahatma Letters, a book of letters from Adepts written to two early Theosophists, refers to another hell, called Avichi. To this, Master Koot Hoomi writes, go the monsters of wickedness who have identified themselves with evil, those who, knowing good and evil, have deliberately chosen evil, loving it for its own sake. They will remain in a state of suffering in Avichi until the end of the *manavantara*, that is, until the present universe goes out of manifestation. Then they will be annihilated.

Leadbeater and Besant, writing of Avichi before the letters were published, state that this is the destination of the magicians of the left hand path who have been working towards the wrong goal of completely separate selfhood. Such an aim is in opposition to the divine plan of ultimate union with God. The zealous, clever magician reaches the target for which he has labored through lifetimes, and has his reward: the utter isolation of Avichi, a state in which he stands absolutely alone, cut off from all life. The heaven he worked for becomes his hell.

While such hells as the Eighth Sphere and Avichi bring great suffering for long periods, they are more merciful than the fire and brimstone hell of the Christians with its everlasting torment.

Sri Yukteswar Giri, who appeared after death in a

materialized body, made some interesting comments to his old pupil, Paramahansa Yogananda, on the hells and better places he had seen in the astral. He stated that there were various vibratory regions for good and evil spirits. The good can travel freely through many regions, while the evil are confined to certain limited zones. The fallen angels expelled from other worlds, he said, dwell in the gloom-drenched regions of the lower astral cosmos, working out their evil *karma*. Among them there is constant friction and many wars are waged.

But in the vast realms above this dark prison are shining and beautiful zones of the astral universe. Here can be found millions of human souls who have come, more or less recently, from the earth. Also in certain areas of the astral are myriads of non-human beings: animals, fairies, goblins, gnomes, demigods, nature spirits and others. This is in agreement with the findings of the Theosophical investigators.

But Sri Yukteswar Giri talks also of a wonderful, illumined astral region which he called Hiranyaloka. Inhabitants here, he said, have already passed through the ordinary astral spheres where people go after death on earth. But they are not yet ready to enter the high causal world. The great *yogi* explained that his work in Hiranyaloka was to help souls prepare themselves for entering the high causal plane.

There is no mention of this special astral region, lying beyond the normal astral plane, in the Theosophical writings. But Sri Yukteswar Giri also calls Hiranyaloka a "heaven"; so perhaps it is one of the sub-planes of Theosophy's mental plane to which the astral dwellers go when they shed their astral bodies.

This transition is known as the astral death, and Theosophical writers say that the astral corpse falls to a particular area, sometimes called the astral cemetery.

A certain amount of mental matter may, however, be left with the shell of the astral or desire body. This happens if thought and desire have been too interwoven and entangled; then a part of the lower mind remains and the astral corpse becomes what is known as a "shade." This retains a life of its own for a time, and can be stimulated to a greater appearance of life under certain circumstances.

Many astral deaths, however, according to Robert Crookall's studies, do not leave any husk, shell or shade. If there has been a progressive refinement and purification as the Higher Self unveils Itself, the astral shell disintegrates when discarded, he says, leaving no discernible form behind.

People have no dread of astral death as many do of the physical death. When the time comes, it is said, they simply go into a drowsy state, into a change of consciousness, and awake to find themselves in the radiant world beyond the astral.

In Theosophical terms this great plane, with its seven sub-planes, is generally known as Devachan. It is also frequently called the heaven worlds. Its seven sub-planes are divided into two main groups, the four lowest being called the mental plane, and the three highest the causal plane. It should be realized, too, that within the seven main divisions of the heavens there are many special zones or locales. Christ said: "In my Father's house are many mansions," but who can say just how many?

Like the earth, the astral, and every other phenomenal world, Devachan is, of course, a creation of consciousness. But as the soul's level of consciousness is now very different from that of earth life, the heavens are not a glorified replica of earth, as much of the astral is.

Investigators who are able to penetrate this far and

see, or even glimpse, the effulgent glory of these regions, realize, like Dante, that they have neither the skill nor the vocabulary to describe them.

Theosophical writers and lecturers have found that when they speak of this high plane, people are inclined to think that it is just a dream world. But, as Annie Besant stresses, it is actually less dreamlike than the earth. It is, she says, two veils closer to the ultimate Reality, the earthly and astral veils having been cast aside. Thus the souls in heaven do not have to see through a glass darkly. The thin gossamer veil of Devachanic matter lets through the glorious beauty and joy of the divine light more copiously. Devachan may be thought of as the seven-ringed outer court to the soul's true spiritual home which is beyond all phenomenal regions.

Who goes to Devachan? The Master Koot Hoomi answers: "All who have not slipped down into the mire of unredeemable sin go there." Some, a very few, go directly there after physical death, but most after a period, long or short, in the astral regions of purgation and purification.

So, all except the loyal servants of evil, who meet annihilation in the hells of the Eighth Sphere or Avichi, go to heaven. But not for eternity. Except at its very highest level, this place of unmixed happiness is temporary. The soul's period there may be long, or it may be short, depending on a number of factors, but it has an ending.

So why do we go there at all? We are all a mixture, in different proportions, of good and bad. Most of the bad is sloughed off in the astral regions. The remainder is concentrated in the astral permanent atom — a *karmic* seed for the next life on earth.

But in the meantime there are some rewards to be collected for our good thoughts, words and deeds in the life recently lived. Here, in Devachan, we reap a tenfold harvest (as the Plato story suggests) for any good we did, for any unselfish actions, for our efforts to transcend desire. Moreover, here we are compensated for wrongs and injustices suffered on earth through group or national *karma* — for no individual fault of our own, so to speak. In this way the scales are balanced.

Apart from such considerations, it is the nature of the soul, in its evolutionary journey, to move towards its spiritual goal, and Devachan is a good step nearer to it than the astral, and two strides nearer than Mother Earth.

Life in the heaven world, as all the scriptures of all the nations teach, is a truly happy one. There is no disharmony, no sorrow, no want, no conflict there. The quality of the happiness changes, of course, and becomes more and more spiritual and divine as consciousness rises through the seven levels. But it is always unalloyed, without the clash of opposites that we know on earth where, as Sai Baba says, pleasure is just an interval between two pains, and evil is always at war with goodness. But on that high plane there is no pain, no evil.

A little introspection will show that here on earth we need the clash of opposites to create a challenge and give zest to life. So, obviously, there must be a tremendous alteration in human consciousness to make the heaven life acceptable, let alone blissful to us.

The length of time each individual spends in Devachan depends on the quality of his former life on earth, and his soul's level of evolutionary progress. It also depends on the development of his consciousness, on how soon he will begin to feel again the need for the struggles and conflicts of earthly life.

Some souls may spend a short time in heaven. Others may spend centuries, or even a thousand years of earth time, there. But Devachanic time is even more subjective than astral time. Life there bears no relationship to our concepts of chronological time and three-dimensional space.

Eventually, however, the soul sheds another illusory veil, albeit an ethereal one, and moves onward from the mental to the causal levels of Devachan. But to the majority of mankind today, Leadbeater says, the causal experience is brief. Also, because their consciousness is not developed to the causal level most people spend their short time here in a dreamy, semi-conscious, but blissful state. Yet for a moment or two they have a flash of waking causal consciousness, and catch a vision of wondrous supernal beauty. Even such a glimpse of this high abode may be enough to inspire great music, poetry or art in their future lives which represent a yearning to recapture the lost horizons of beauty and splendor briefly seen, then lost again.

At a little higher level, fully awake, are those who have earnestly tried to live the spiritual life on earth; they have stored most of their treasures in heaven, to use Christ's analogy, but they still have a few treasures remaining on earth, and will eventually return there.

At the highest level, the apex of the phenomenal worlds, we come to the "seventh heaven." None who have glimpsed it will ever attempt to describe this divine realm. "Once heard," wrote a mystic, "the harmony of this mystic world is never forgotten — its memories remain to strengthen us in moments of trial and sorrow."

The souls who dwell here, it is said, are able to carry their memories back unbroken from one past incarnation to another. They are fully aware of the personalities in which they played out their series of lives, and can read them, like a book of one act plays. They understand God's evolutionary plan for them as individuals, and see their lives as steps in that plan, leading them to where they are now, at the inmost court of the Divine Eternal Home. This must be the heaven of which Christ spoke.

There are no treasures left stored up on earth, no desires or *karmic* debts to call these souls back. Some, indeed, will go back to earth but only for the purpose of teaching or otherwise helping mankind. Those who do not thus return voluntarily through brotherly love and compassion, will move on into the bliss of *nirvana*, the indescribable union with the Divine.

But very few souls climb after physical death to this top of the fourteen-rung ladder. Most, before reaching it, will return to earth, says Theosophy. Why? The main reason is that they still desire to go back: they still have that thirst for sentient life known as *trishna*. While a trace of *trishna* remains, "they will come back, come back as long as the red earth rolls," as Kipling expressed it.

And coming back, they bring with them their stored up tendencies and attachments, their *karmic* debts to be paid, their packages of good and bad, of pain and pleasure.

In a deeper sense, too, while a soul has *trishna*, it has not finished its evolutionary journey. It has not torn away the veils of ignorance and realized its true divine identity. It has not attained the purpose for which it began its long pilgrimage through the phenomenal worlds.

Various Theosophical books describe in some detail the *modus operandi* of rebirth. But, in general terms, here is what takes place for the average person. The return journey begins from the causal plane. Passing through the mental and astral planes, the reincarnating entity, clothed in its causal body, draws about it the matter of these planes. This is not done consciously, but takes place automatically. The matter thus gathered during the downward journey will be appropriate to the type of mental and astral bodies required for the particular life about to begin. The ethereal matter is not shaped to human form immediately, but is held as a cloud, within or around the causal body, which is, itself, ovoid in shape — somewhat like a Shiva *lingam*.

Entities returning to earth through the mental and astral planes, not having formed mental and causal bodies, presumably do not have any contact with the normal dwellers on those planes who are on the upward path. Indeed, the "transit camps" of the travellers on the downward journey may be in an entirely different division of those vast realms. Should the inhabitants see them at all, perhaps from a distance, it may be just as shining ovoid shapes — moving swiftly, like the "shooting stars" that Er saw from the banks of the Lethe.

Before entering the earth plane the entity must pass through a barrier where the vibrations of its consciousness are considerably lowered. Once beyond that "consciousness barrier" — symbolized by the classical River of Forgetfulness — the soul forgets its recent existence on the inner planes, and its former life on earth.

As suggested by the Plato story, we do apparently have some choice of the parents and conditions of our new life. But only the progressed souls will choose wisely, it seems. Undeveloped souls, saturated with strong *trishna*, will most likely dash blindly into the first rebirth opening that presents itself. But *karmic* laws and other factors governing the question of rebirth are really a great mystery.

Human experience and parapsychological research offer a good deal of evidence that not all rebirth scenarios follow the average pattern. For one reason or another, some souls reincarnate quickly, without going through long periods in the inner worlds. Children who die inadvertently, for example, sometimes do so. Advanced souls who wish to come back without delay, in order to carry on an important spiritual mission, will do so.

In such cases the entity may bring back its former subtle vehicles much as they were in the previous life. This is a reason why some children remember their last earth lives in great detail. There has not been a tremendous change in the vibration rate of consciousness from the causal down to the earth level.

There are cases on record, too, though comparatively rare, where people who died as adults, and spent a century or more on the higher planes before rebirth, remember much of their former earth lives. The classical poet would say they had not drunk deeply enough of the waters of Lethe.

One of the most remarkable cases of such past life remembrances, collected and thoroughly investigated by the well known researcher on reincarnation, Dr. Ian Stevenson (a psychiatrist who has carefully investigated memories of past lives), is that of Edward Ryall. This Englishman recalls in vivid detail his life as a yeoman farmer named John Fletcher in the seventeenth century. Fletcher, who lived in Somerset, took part in the Monmouth Rebellion and the Battle of Sedgemoor, and had a love affair with a woman named Melanie which ended sadly. He remembers being killed in 1685 by a cavalryman in the army of James II. In 1902, two hundred and seventeen years later, Fletcher was reborn as Edward Ryall.

Dr. Stevenson found that Ryall's account of seventeenth century life in England was astonishingly accurate. Furthermore, it included many obscure details that only rare studies of the period would give.

About his own memories Ryall says they "are as much an integral part of my mind as are my recollections of my present life. They are present in my waking consciousness and are not the product of any effort of profound recall, except when I wish to clear up a point which has become vague or doubtful."

Ryall has written a book about his memories, entitled *Born Twice — Total Recall of a Seventeenth Century Life*, and Stevenson has spent years checking the memories against little known historical facts found in obscure records. He remarks that Ryall's memories should command the attention of future historians of Restoration England, for he reveals many intimate details of life in that period.

After evaluating the wealth of evidence, Dr. Stevenson concludes that the verisimilitude and detailed accuracy of the memories of Edward Ryall have "contributed not a little to the slowly accumulating evidence for reincarnation."

Several books by Leadbeater, Besant, and others of the Theosophical movement give considerable detail about life and conditions on those higher planes where the human soul spends a greater proportion of its time than it does down here. Also explained in detail are the why and how and when of its return to earth.

But there have been other occult investigations into life beyond the border, and we will see how these compare with the general Theosophical concepts.

Some Rosicrucian Concepts

A good Rosicrucian friend of mine let his head-quarters in California know that I wished, if possible, to include some Rosicrucian concepts of life after death in this comparative study. As a result, they kindly sent me a copy of the book *Mansions of the Soul* by H. Spencer Lewis, saying that this contained the essential teachings on the subject. The quotations and ideas given here are from that book.

Like the Theosophists, the Rosicrucians teach that man is one with the divine essence, which they call the Oversoul. In their words, we are essentially undivided segments of the Oversoul. At the same time, infused into the segment, or somehow in close association with it, we have an individual soul.

In the transition called death the withdrawal of the soul from the physical body may take from ten minutes to half an hour, and sometimes longer. Then the soul may for a time stay around its former habitat — for various reasons connected with earthly interests and desires. While there, it may be seen or sensed by people with a gift of clairvoyance.

Soon, or after some time, the soul is drawn upward into the spiritual or cosmic realms. There it dwells in one or another of the twelve "mansions of the soul" — mansion being the name given to a main division of the cosmic realm.

While in these zones, the souls retain the dominant features of their recent personalities on earth. Even their names from that incarnation are retained for the period as identification symbols. Memories of earlier earth lives, with the names they had then, are vaguely there in the background of their consciousness, rather like the memories of childhood.

But life is not spent idly in the mansions. The souls there are instructed in divine knowledge to purge them of the former errors for which they repent. Thus, as time passes, through knowledge and divine grace, they become more purified and more evolved.

But, though purged of many blots on their characters, the souls realize that they must return to earth to make amends for the errors they made while there. They become "keenly aware of their previous mistakes, and the repentance and regret in their hearts, and their burning desire to undo the wrongs they have done, and make compensation, constitute the factors and conditions which men have been pleased to call Hell and Purgatory."

But though they suffer for their sins in these conditions, they must still compensate for them on earth. "For," Lewis says, "it is the flesh that has committed the sin and it is the flesh that must compensate through suffering." Therefore the soul must be reborn.

It is one of the enigmas inherent in the doctrine of *karma* that man cannot adequately make amends for errors made on earth in realms other than earth. Whatever he may suffer in purgatory or hell, if he is to pluck out the weeds of ignorance and error, he must come back to the earthly soil in which the seeds were sown.

Theosophy and Hinduism also teach that there is suffering for errors both in the purgatories of the inner planes and back on earth in a new life. Such double sufferings may not seem reasonable, but suffering can be a spur to progress, and whatever advances we may make in the astral realm, we must learn the lessons needed for character development and spiritual evolution back in the hard schoolroom of earth.

The Rosicrucians say that each soul has a definite cycle of rebirths, with periods of non-physical existence in between. The length of these periods between incarnations varies greatly; occasionally it is brief, but generally the soul spends many years, even centuries, in the cosmic realms. The main purpose of the intervals between births is to permit the soul "to further purify itself and become illumined by the Divine Mind and Cosmic Wisdom. "

Rosicrucian teachings and Theosophy seem to agree on general lines about the soul's destiny after death. The main difference between them lies in their classification of the after-death realms. The Rosicrucians talk of twelve "mansions of the soul," whereas the Theosophical investigators, Leadbeater and Besant, divided the realm into two planes and fourteen sub-planes. Madame H. P. Blavatsky, in *The Secret Doctrine*, wrote of three main *lokas* (places) beyond the earth. In Vol. V, she writes that the first *loka* above the earth has three types of matter interpenetrating: etheric, astral and mental; the next *loka* has astral and mental matter only; and the *loka* beyond that is of purely mental matter.

All matter, of any type, is objective to the consciousness at its own level. "Matter, existing in supersensuous states, is fully objective to the spiritual eye of man, as a horse or tree is to the ordinary mortal." (*The Secret Doctrine*, 11:239).

"On the inner planes," writes E. L. Gardner, "it is the *rupa devas* who do the building. They build the pattern of thought as quickly as we think it. So there are innumerable spheres, places, *lokas*, in the next world built to represent the thoughts of millions of people, both about the after-life, and also ordinary thinking about ordinary living."*

*See *The Wider View, Studies in the Secret Doctrine* by E. L. Gardner.

The Secret Doctrine also describes the *talas* that go downward. They are of coarser vibration, and therefore of denser matter, than the earth. *Tala I* is near the surface of the earth and to a degree overlaps it. Ghosts are sometimes seen in this *tala* and to the human eyes appear silvery grey, like mist. *Tala II* is physically denser than this, and *Tala III* deeper still into heaviness, sensuality, selfishness and cruelty, a veritable "hell."

"At the 'nethermost pit'," writes Gardner, "there is *atala* (no place) where forms that have become separated from their spiritual principle are ground to fragments and reduced again to pure elemental essence." This probably corresponds to Leadbeater's Eighth Sphere.

But such differences of classification are not important. The only way of charting the territories of the undiscovered country is to go there superconsciously, to make a complete exploration and bring back the detailed memories into waking consciousness. No easy task this, for even the greatest seers and occultists. Their penetration and observations may vary; their powers of astral and Devachanic memory will be different, their understanding, interpretation and methods of classification will depend a great deal on their different cultural backgrounds.

On the difficulty of interpreting the supersensuous worlds, Master Koot Hoomi wrote: "These subjects are only partly for understanding. A higher faculty belonging to the higher life must see — and it is truly impossible to force it upon one's understanding merely in words."

Madame Blavatsky echoed this, saying that it was impossible to obtain a cut and dried, clear account of the mysteries of birth and death, and that the destiny of the human soul was too subtle and intricate to be expressed in straightforward language.

We must, therefore, keep an open mind. Views through different clairvoyant windows and doorways will give us varying panoramas of the undiscovered country. But this is all to the good. It will prevent us from arriving across the border when the time comes with clear cut, neatly parcelled ideas that may be wrong. It will help us to get the general concepts and broad principles right, and be prepared for whatever particulars present themselves.

In the company of Swedenborg we get another, exhilarating view of the elusive land.

Through the Swedenborg Door

In the century before organized psychic research, and the Theosophical Society, there lived in Sweden a citizen of high repute who became one of the most brilliant seers in modern times.

Born in 1688, Emmanuel Swedenborg was the son of an eminent Lutheran bishop. His early interests lay in the direction of science, mathematics and philosophy. After leaving university at the age of twenty-one, he lived in England and various continental countries for some years. There he studied mathematics and astronomy with some of the notable men of his day, such as Halley and Flamsteed. When he was twenty-seven he was appointed to a position on the Board of Mines, the State department responsible for the supervision of the mining industry in Sweden.

Apart from serving with great renown in this high government position for over thirty years, he had many other interests and attained eminence in science, mathematics and practical affairs. He spoke nine languages and wrote 150 works in seventeen sciences. As a mining engineer, he reproduced the first exhaustive works on metallurgy. In mathematics he developed the first Swedish texts on algebra and the calculus. Physiology and anatomy were among his many research pursuits, and he discovered the functions of several areas of the brain. Among his inventions were a glider, an undersea boat and an ear trumpet for the deaf.

Swedenborg was a distinguished philosopher, arriving at some philosophic concepts very close to Vedanta with which he had no contact whatever. The fundamental principle of his philosophy is the substantial reality of the spiritual, the material world being a fallacy of the senses. In truth, he maintained, the only substance is God from whom all created things derive their being. It is foolish, he thought, to say that God created the universe out of nothing; all things are derived from God, Himself. But God, in His inmost essence, is incomprehensible to both men and angels.

In science, Swedenborg's vision was ahead of his time. Whereas Newton, his great contemporary, thought of matter as composed of impenetrable atoms endowed from without with motion, Swedenborg propounded the theory that within the atom were discrete orders of particles, each order built from a higher, more energetic order, and each particle endowed from within with motion of a closed vortical nature. The smallest particles have virtually no dimensions, but, by spiralling around a center at infinite speeds, give the appearance of solidity to matter. The resemblance of this theory to the modern concept of the atom is remarkable indeed.

Swedenborg, being the eldest son of a noble family, had a seat in the House of Nobles. He often dined with royalty, yet when in England he lodged with tradesmen and joined in their family lives, even learning several useful trades this way. Thus he seemed to fulfill one of the Kipling requisites for the true man, who can "walk with kings nor lose the common touch."

In his time the Board of Mines consisted of two Councillors at the top and six Assessors. Swedenborg was one of the Assessors. When one of the Councillors was about to retire, Swedenborg, who was then fifty-nine years of age, was offered this greatly prized post. But a wonderful new dimension had come into his life by then.

Four years earlier his spiritual sight had begun to open, revealing the realm beyond death. This intromission into the spirit world had increased, and for two years before the offer of official promotion, he had been holding frequent conversations with spirits and angels. The conversations, he said, were "as man to man."

From his intercourse with high beings, he felt himself called to a great mission that would require all his time and energy. The most important part of this mission, he believed, was to explain the spiritual meaning of the scriptures. But another aspect — and one that interests us here — was to investigate the nature of life after death. His developing spiritual sight was revealing to him a hereafter very different from the one propounded in the churches of his day. So he felt that he had been called by God to bring new truths to men in matters concerning the destiny of the spirit.

This great mission was, he knew, much more important than worldly honors and advantages. And so he wrote to the Swedish King, asking leave to decline the offer of the position of Councillor, and to be allowed to retire from the Board on a life pension. His requests were granted, and he was commended on the fidelity and renown with which he had carried out his official duties for over thirty years.

From his retirement in 1747 until his death in 1772 he spent his time on spiritual investigations, and writing about his discoveries. Apart from his work as a member of Parliament, and his genial but infrequent intercourse with friends, he gave up the affairs of the world. He remained vigorous and healthy in mind and body for the whole of his life, even, so it is said, growing a new set of teeth at the age of eighty-one.

Some of his critics say that his visions of the other worlds were hallucinatory — just mental aberrations. But apart from the known facts of his life, and his keen, practical mind, which show no signs whatever of mental imbalance, there is strong evidence that many of his clairvoyant visions, concerning both this world and the next, were factually correct. A few examples may help the reader to form a judgement about the objective reality of Swedenborg's visions.

The famous philosopher Immanuel Kant, who was very interested in Swedenborg's strange gifts, wrote (in a letter to a friend) an account of one well attested event involving extrasensory perception. At four o'clock one Saturday afternoon Swedenborg arrived in Gothenburg from England. "Mr. William Castel invited him to his house, together with a party of fifteen persons. About six o'clock Swedenborg went out, and returned to the company, looking quite pale and alarmed. He said that a fire had just broken out in the city of Stockholm (Gothenburg is about three hundred miles from Stockholm), and that it was spreading very fast. He was restless and went outside often. He stated that the house of one of his friends, whom he named, was already in ashes, and that his own house was in danger. At eight o'clock, after he had been out again, he joyfully exclaimed, 'Thank God the fire is extinguished, the third door from my house!' " The news occasioned great commotion throughout Gothenburg. It was announced to the Governor the same evening.

Questioned by the Governor, Swedenborg gave full details about the fire. Two days later, a messenger came from Stockholm, and the royal courier arrived at the Governor's house. Letters carried by both messengers described how the fire had started, the damage done and when and where it was extinguished. The details agreed with those which Swedenborg had given at the time it happened. The fire was extinguished at eight o'clock, just as he had described to his friends in Gothenburg.

Seeing into other dimensions and talking to the souls of the dead seemed to Swedenborg as easy, or easier, than observing events at a distance on earth.

"I have been allowed," he said, "to talk with practically everyone I have ever known during his physical life — with some for hours, with some for weeks or months, with some for years — all for the overriding purpose that I might be assured of this fact, and might bear witness to it."

Many great and eminent people of his time bore witness to his ability. One was the Queen of Sweden. Count Hopken gives this account of the incident. Swedenborg was one day at a Court reception. Asking him about things in the other life, Her Majesty enquired, casually it seemed, if he had seen there her deceased brother, the late Prince Royal of Prussia. When he said that he had not, Her Majesty requested him to try to see her dear brother and give him her greetings. Swedenborg promised to do so. At another reception, a week later, Swedenborg again came to Court and gave the Queen a startling message. He had, he said, seen her deceased brother in the other world. The brother sent his greetings and his apologies for not having answered the Queen's last letter. But he would do so now, through Swedenborg. The answer, transmitted by Swedenborg, had a very profound effect on the Queen. Some said she almost fainted. To Swedenborg she exclaimed, "No one except God knows this secret."

Apparently the ladies around the Queen when she received the message did not hear the details, or if they did, they kept silent on the matter. It had not been known in Sweden that the Queen had, during the war with Prussia, been carrying on a correspondence with her brother who was a prince of the enemy country. This was no doubt the reason why in subsequent days many carriages stopped at Swedenborg's door, and some of the first gentlemen of the kingdom entered his house. They wanted to know the message that had so startled and upset the Queen. But Swedenborg, faithful to a promise that he had apparently given Her Majesty, did not reveal the secret.

The next story also comes from the pen of Immanuel Kant who had commissioned a friend to investigate the matter on the spot.

The widow of the Dutch ambassador to Stockholm, some time after the death of her husband, was called upon by a goldsmith to pay for a silver service which her husband had purchased from him. The widow felt sure that her husband had himself paid the debt, but she could not find the receipt. Because the amount was considerable, the widow, in great distress, requested Swedenborg to ask her deceased husband about it. He promised to do so. Three days later he called at the widow's house where there was, at the time, some company having coffee.

In his calm way Swedenborg informed the lady that he had conversed with her late husband. The debt, the husband said, had been paid seven months before his death and the receipt was in a bureau in a room upstairs. The widow replied that the bureau had been searched thoroughly, and that the receipt had not been found among the papers there. Swedenborg then said that her husband had explained to him exactly how a certain secret compartment in the bureau could be located, and that the receipt, along with his private Dutch correspondence, would be found in that compartment. Upon hearing this the whole company moved upstairs; the bureau was opened; and, to the great astonishment and excitement of all, the secret compartment was found. It contained the important receipt and private correspondence.

Swedenborg's descriptions and assessments of the realms beyond death are in agreement with the main features brought out by the great occultists and modern psychic researchers. There are, however, some differences in the details.

Writing about death and the immediate state thereafter, Swedenborg says, in *True Christian Religion*: "As soon as they are deceased and revive as to the spirit, which takes place generally on the third day after the heart has ceased to beat, they appear to themselves in a body similar to the one they had in the world, so that they do not know but that they are still living there; yet it is not a material body, but a substantial one, though to their senses it appears like a material one. After some days they see that they are in a world where there are various societies instituted, which is called 'The World of Spirits', and is in the middle between heaven and hell."

When they are convinced that they have died,

people are amazed because everything is so different from what they had expected according to church teachings. Some are, indeed, angry that they were not told by their religious leaders what to expect after death. If they were atheists, they are at first bewildered and embarrassed.

Coming into the world of spirits, and looking much as they did on earth, they are easily recognized by friends already there, and there are many happy reunions. Husbands and wives may come together if they wish, and will stay together for a longer or shorter time according to the truth of their love.

In this intermediate region, corresponding perhaps to some of the sub-planes of the astral as described by the occultists, the spirits at the beginning lead a life very similar to the one they led in the world. But very soon they meet ministering "Angels of Light" who teach and guide them.

The Judgement, or Review, is dramatized as a memory book from which is read out an account of the person's every deed, word and thought from the moment of birth to the moment of death in the world. In this all the people concerned (or perhaps thought-forms of them) are called up to bear witness at the scene of judgement. As every feeling involved in the actual life experiences is felt again, this moment of truth is a devastating exercise in self-analysis and self-judgement.

Refuting the church doctrine of the sleep in the grave until the final Resurrection and Judgement Day, Swedenborg says: "The time of everyone's resurrection is when he dies." "Every man takes with him his memory," and these memories appear, when called forth, "as though they were read from a book."

Thus in essence the person passes judgement on his own past life — which is in agreement with the occult teachings and the indications of modern research.

Swedenborg understood the world of spirits was divided into three main sections, as were also, he thought, the heaven realms above and the hell regions beneath. He states that spirits in the intermediate zone can make progress towards greater purity and higher levels of being. In *Divine Providence* he writes: "There is also given to all men after death the opportunity of amending their life if they can; they are instructed and led by the Lord, acting through the instrumentality of angels, and, as they then know that they are living after death, and that there is a heaven and a hell, they at first assent to truths; but those who, while in the world, did not believe in God nor shun evils as sins, after a short time feel a repugnance for truth and reject it."

The latter type turn their faces towards a life that is more congenial to their taste. As people remain the same after death as before, we can understand this reaction against spirituality by some. There are many here who enjoy the bars and brothels and wallow in the desire-world, but would consider it a great pain and penance to attend a church service, or listen to any kind of spiritual instruction. So too in the world of spirits there are many who gravitate towards their own loves and interests. Some of the great sinners will be ready to learn and turn their faces heavenward, but others will find the whole idea of purity, spirituality and the unselfish life of heaven repugnant to them.

The difference between this world and that is that there the "sheep," by their own inclination, become divided from the "goats." Hypocrisy is no longer possible there. What one is within shows clearly. The outward appearance takes on and reflects the inner nature. The faces of those who move towards the heaven of truth and bliss acquire a wonderful, shining, spiritual beauty. Those sliding down the slippery slope towards hell grow more gross and repugnant in appearance.

Hell, Swedenborg states, is not from the Lord but from evil itself, "since evil is so joined with its own punishment that they cannot be separated. The Lord casts no one into hell; but every one casts himself thither, both while he lives in the world and also after death when he comes among spirits." This is, of course, the law of *Karma*, expressed in a different way.

A pastor of the New Church, which teaches the Swedenborg doctrines, made this further comment to me: "It is God's mercy that permits souls to go where they desire to go, that is, to hell, and to remain there as long as they wish."

"Did Swedenborg believe that hell is eternal?" I asked the pastor.

"He is not very clear on that point, but he does say that evil spirits are 'punished that thus they may be deterred from doing evil' — which suggests that they may leave hell when they have learned their lesson and are ready for living the higher life." This is confirmed by another statement by Swedenborg: that the Lord delivers a soul from hell "so far as he does not will and love to abide in his own evil."

So, perhaps, we can understand Swedenborg's hell to be a place where people go of their own free will, where they can wallow in their own desires and sins until they learn that such a life brings more pain and punishment than pleasure. Thus, while being a place of just punishment, hell is also a place of correction and rehabilitation. This concept is in keeping with our image of God as a loving Father, and as a Shepherd who, while the ninety- and-nine lambs are safely in the fold, goes out on the "mountains wild and bare" to search for the one that is lost.

Furthermore, the idea of the final redemption of all souls is in keeping with the great seer's basic philosophic concept, that God is the one and only Reality, and that all souls derive their being and nature from Him. All souls are part of the one eternal Substance, God. How then can any be condemned to everlasting torment or annihilation?

At the other end of the scale from hell are the glorious heaven realms. It appears from his writings that Swedenborg's spiritual sight was opened sufficiently for him to penetrate into these realms, at least to some degree.

Brought up in the Christian tradition, he calls the dwellers in heaven angels, and says that all angels were once human beings. The Great Mahatmas, writing to Sinnett a hundred years later, are in agreement with this idea. They state that *devas* (angels) are former human beings.

The angels, according to Swedenborg, have reached heaven as a result of the lives they lived on earth, though most have also required a period of training and purification in the intermediate world of spirits. In general, angels do not see what is going on in this world. Modern Spiritualism has formed the same conclusion; the vibrational gap between this world and the heaven realms is so great that the heaven dwellers do not perceive the activities of earth. Nevertheless, there does seem to be, according to most occult and religious teachings, a class of angels, or *devas*, specially assigned to assist in man's spiritual development.

Swedenborg portrays a heaven that sings its song deep in the heart of man. Love, as Christ taught, is the one most important ingredient of the heaven-aspiring, heaven-attaining life. But it must be true love; not the kind that has a selfish hope of reward, but the love that loves for its own sake.

The seer was, however, at odds with his church on certain features of the heaven life. According to church theology heaven was an escape from work, and the only activities of the angels seemed to be playing harps and singing before the throne of God. But Swedenborg maintained that there were no idlers in heaven. All were engaged on some useful task — not for the sake of their own gain but for performing something useful in promoting the happiness of others. The kinds of occupation are various and diverse. The work performed by one angel is never exactly the same as that performed by another, "and, therefore, the delight of one angel is not exactly the same as the delight of another." It seems that, although the emphasis is on unity and cooperation in the heaven life, individual uniqueness remains.

The churches of his day taught that, unless a child was baptized, it could not go to heaven. But Swedenborg denied this patently unjust and cruel teaching. All little children who die throughout the whole world, whether in the church or out of it, are, he said, raised up by the Lord to heaven. There they are instructed by the angels, who take care of them. This continues until, as they advance in wisdom, they grow to maturity. In fact, he said, a third of the population of heaven consists of children.

Moreover, in opposition to church teaching that there is no marriage in heaven, Swedenborg writes that two married partners may meet and continue their life together as long as they wish. With some it will be a short time, with others a long time. "As love that is truly conjugal endures to eternity, it follows that the wife becomes more and more a wife and the husband more and more a husband." While such marriage partnerships make for greater mutual happiness, they will continue.

All beings in the higher spiritual realms throw off old age, which really belonged to the body only, and attain to the gladsome springtime of youth. They maintain their youth, with a beauty surpassing anything the mortal mind can conceive, for all time, unto eternity.

The reader will note that, unlike Plato, the Rosicrucians, the Theosophists, the ancient mystery religions and other esoteric teachings, Swedenborg says nothing about the return of the soul to earth after a period spent in the heavens or hells. He always spoke what he believed to be the truth boldly, without fear of consequences, so we can take it that he found no evidence of reincarnation in his clairvoyant penetration of the inner regions. I have heard students of the deeper occult teachings say that Swedenborg was, therefore, wrong in his spiritual perception and his understanding of the soul's destiny. But something is not necessarily wrong because incomplete. The spiritual truths we can know while incarnate are only partial truths for, as St. Paul said, "Now we see through a glass darkly."

The truths that Swedenborg was permitted to perceive and transmit were controlled no doubt by the great Masters of Wisdom, and perhaps the time was not right for the West to be reintroduced to the doctrine of rebirth in the eighteenth century. The opposition to revelations about the hereafter, and his new interpretation of Biblical texts, was quite violent enough without that. So whether reincarnation is a true doctrine or not — and I personally believe it is — Swedenborg found no clues to it in his spiritual journeys.

As spiritualistic communications have shown, discarnate souls can be a long time in the astral plane, and presumably also in the heaven world, without themselves knowing of reincarnation. Swedenborg's vision probably did not extend to the causal plane from which souls incarnate and know — albeit sometimes for a short period — that they are going to be reborn on earth.

Nor should those comparing the teachings about life after death, coming from different sources, be too concerned about the different ways of classifying, numbering and naming the divisions of the realms beyond death. Swedenborg, for example, divided the intermediate world of spirits into three parts, whereas Theosophy divides the astral plane (which probably corresponds approximately to the world of spirits) into seven sub-planes. Likewise Swedenborg writes of three divisions of heaven, while Theosophy again makes the number of sub-planes seven.

The same phenomena can easily be divided into either three or seven parts. Take, for instance, man himself. Madame Blavatsky, in her early writings, presented man as a triad (physical body, revitalizing astral body and immortal spirit). This is a legitimate and easily understood classification. In her later writings, however, she went a step further and divided the human compound into seven principles, or, to use modern terms, seven fields of energy.

Perhaps the astral plane and the mental (heaven) plane can be likewise each classified correctly into three or seven or a different number of parts, depending on the viewer, his background, the angle from which he views the phenomena, and the depth of his probe. The subdivisions, it is said by the occultists, often merge into one another, and are not always clearly defined.

Summarizing information gleaned on this subject from Spiritualism, Dr. Robert Crookall writes: "There are many mansions. Communicators say that the various spheres or planes are not sharply divided off and to some extent interpenetrate each other. The first sphere closely resembles the earth. The second is a slight advance on this. The third, called by many names (Paradise, Summerland, Elysium, etc.), is a glorified earth. Beyond are higher spheres that are indescribable."

6

Spiritualism: Informed Views and Warnings

The two founders of the Theosophical movement, Madame Blavatsky and Colonel H. S. Olcott, both spent some years investigating modern Spiritualism, which had made its appearance in America in the late 1840's, and spread quickly over the western world. Olcott examined and tested much phenomena in the United States while he was still a young man. Blavatsky, who had great psychic gifts herself, studied Spiritualism in Russia and other countries, including Egypt. Finally, in partnership, they both carried out considerable research in America on the subject.

Both, by the time they launched the Theosophical Society in 1875, had come to certain conclusions. They had found that, though there was a good deal of mediumistic cheating, there were some genuine mediums producing genuine phenomena. Some of this phenomena, they thought (as did the researchers who came later), originated in the unconscious minds of the mediums or any sitters present. Much of it, on the other hand, they concluded, came from impersonators on the other side of the veil, and that only a little of the mass of communications was, in fact, from the actual discarnate spirits who claimed to be speaking.

This element of deception by beings on the other side figures largely in Theosophical and other thought, but it does not seem to have concerned the modern psychic researchers much, if at all. To understand who or what such spirit impostors might be, we must consider the import of certain terms used by Theosophists and some other occultists.

At the second death, when the immortal soul withdraws into the heaven worlds, it may leave behind a form of astral body which has been the vehicle of the person's lower desires. The soul takes with it into the heaven regions only the higher parts of the mind. So that, remaining behind with the astral body, will be a degree of lower mentality and memory, closely interwoven with the desire mechanism.

The degree of mentality left with the astral vehicle varies with different individuals. If there is very little, what remains is called an astral 'shell.' If there is more consciousness and memory, the remaining entity is known as a 'shade' or 'specter.' Both these types of astral remains — the shell and the shade — will disintegrate sooner or later and vanish. A shell will break up more quickly than a shade.

Besides these, there are other types of entities moving about in the lower astral. There are, for instance, artificial elementals which are really thought-forms produced by living people on earth, either intentionally or otherwise. It is said that fictional characters, into which much intensive, concentrated thought has gone, gain a vivid reality as thought-forms in the astral. Some of Dickens' characters, for instance, became astral entities and, reportedly, troubled their creator at times.

Artificial elementals, created intentionally, are usually born in the mind of a powerful magician — black or white. Depending on the purposes of their creators, such entities can be malignant or protective. They can last for long periods if enough vital energy and will power have been put into their creation.

Another class on the astral plane are nature spirits or natural elementals. They have varying degrees of intelligence, can be tricky, deceitful and mischievous, but are seldom malicious.

All the above types of entities can communicate at a spiritualist séance. The true shell can only manifest when galvanized into action by the medium's aura, or when occupied and used by an artificial entity. In the former case the only intelligence it shows comes from the medium; in the latter case it is nearly always malevolent and may be demonic.

A shade frequently communicates at séances. It possesses part of the memory and some idiosyncrasies of the deceased person, and can easily be mistaken for the real soul. It may not itself be conscious of any deception, believing that it is what it claims to be: the spirit of the person whose name it gives through the medium. Those sitters who knew the real person, however, will usually feel that there is something missing, something wrong.

According to Theosophy, much of the phenomena of the séance room are due to the vagaries and inanities of elementals or nature spirits. These are capable of giving messages through raps on furniture, tilting tables, producing "spirit lights," reading the thoughts of those present, and even producing materializations.

Madame Blavatsky, who had clairvoyant vision, stated that when the presence of any soul she wished to contact was announced by a medium, she was never able to see that particular soul among the hosts of spooks that surrounded the medium. "In all the years of my experience I never succeeded in identifying, in one single instance, those I wanted to see. It was only in my dreams and personal visions that I was brought into direct contact with my own blood relatives and friends."

She stated that in the invisible world around us there are many "non-repentant souls, unprogressed and malign spirits — the demons of Christendom, creatures without a soul, without conscience, without responsibility, as well as without light." All too often it is one of these that communicates in the name of a relative or friend. Turning her back on Spiritualism, Blavatsky declared that it was materialistic and necromantic.

The Mahatma Koot Hoomi, who was one of Madame Blavatsky's teachers, says, in a letter to Sinnett, that the normal person, being asleep or in a dreamy lethargic state of consciousness while in the lower astral levels near the earth, is not able to communicate. The only ones really awake in the lower zone, and able to communicate with earth, are people who died violently: by accident, suicide, murder, war or some other form of sudden death. The Mahatma seems to use the term 'shell' to include 'shade,' and says that most of the communications in Spiritualistic circles are from shells. When, however, the soul of a deceased person stays in the astral plane for several years, a living person (usually while asleep) may go to such souls and hold intercourse. Such communion, or intercourse, is easier at this stage than when the soul of the dead reaches the heaven worlds.

Later on, both Leadbeater and Besant had something to say on the subject of Spiritualistic communication through mediums. Leadbeater, who had been a student of Spiritualism before joining the Theosophical Society, came to a conclusion that differed somewhat from that of Madame Blavatsky. He stated, and with this Annie Besant agreed, that a distinct majority of communications in the séance rooms were from departed spirits, as they themselves claimed. A proportion was, however, from shells, shades and impostors on the other side, he said.

Though Spiritualism has done some harm, Leadbeater states, it has probably on the whole done more good. To specify the harm first, he explained that communication tends to hold souls back near the earth and to stimulate their desires for sentient existence, when they should in fact be cutting their earthly ties and moving upward to higher states.

Several harmful effects can come to the living, too. Because it is much easier for spirits to communicate from lower astral planes, it is from there that most messages come. Among the communicators there is a proportion of shades and shells, all of them vampires, drawing vital energy from living people in the séance room. That, incidentally, is why mediums and sitters are often left physically depleted. Moreover, there is always the grave danger of a spook attaching itself to, or even taking possession of, a sitter who is of correspondingly low development, and not strongly integrated.

Spiritualism can easily become nothing more than worship of the dead (necromancy) and worship of the ancestors. And, as Lord Krishna said, those who worship the ancestors will go to the ancestors. If they aim higher, however, towards union with the Divine, they will progress further spiritually. They will still be able to contact their loved ones on lower planes and help to raise them to higher, happier states.

Leadbeater believed that, despite these drawbacks and dangers, the Spiritualistic movement had done much good. It had, for instance, led thousands of sceptics to a belief in life after death. It had also been instrumental in helping many lost bewildered souls who had been suddenly thrown out of their bodies in death, and did not understand what had happened, or where they were.

It is interesting to note, too, that Leadbeater claimed there was a higher spiritualism about which the general public hears nothing. In its circles the same groups of people meet over and over again. No outsider is admitted to upset the vibrations. The results obtained, he said, are often very surprising and enlightening, while the thought-forms that come into being around the center of the meetings are "calculated to raise the mental and spiritual levels of the district."

C. W. Leadbeater, a clergyman of the Church of England before he joined the Theosophical Society, and a bishop of the Liberal Catholic Church during the latter years of his Theosophical work, was not, however, confined to the activities of Spiritualism, even at its highest levels. As we saw in earlier pages, through his clairvoyance and seership he was able to construct a broader and more penetrating picture of the after-death states than is gained through spirit communication.

Once, in conversation with Geoffrey Hodson, another remarkable Theosophical clairvoyant, the writer brought up the problem of Spiritualism, and the differing opinions of the Theosophical leaders on this question. Did Hodson, I asked, agree with Madame Blavatsky that the vast majority of communicators were shells, shades, suicides, or nonhuman entities of some kind, or with Leadbeater who held that most were genuine departed spirits.

"I agree that many are genuine, but even so, perhaps the majority are not what they claim to be. But with clairvoyant sight one always knows which are genuine spirits and which are shells or shades."

"How?" I asked.

"By the eyes. When the immortal soul has departed, the eyes of the resulting shell or shade look quite dead. The true spirit still has the spark of life shining in the eyes."

Remembering the change in a person's eyes immediately the soul leaves the physical body at death, I understood what he meant.

Geoffrey Hodson, like Swedenborg and Leadbeater, did not need the offices of a medium in order to "talk with spirits." He was able to see them as well as converse. But in a séance, when the medium is in a trance and none of the sitters are clairvoyant enough to see the eyes, it is difficult to discriminate between a genuine discarnate soul and a shade or some other entity.

The opinions of some of the Theosophical leaders, such as Leadbeater, on the subject of communication with the dead through mediums are not unlike those of the Roman Catholic Church, as expressed by the Reverend Herbert Thurston, S. J., in his booklet, *Spiritualism*. He writes there: "Though many Catholics incline to the belief that all the genuine phenomena of Spiritualism are the work of demons, it cannot be maintained that this is a part of the Church's official teaching."

He goes on to say that the Church has not pronounced a judgement on the essential nature of Spiritualistic phenomena, but it does believe that in such manifestations diabolic agencies may intervene at times by accident. The Church, therefore, forbids the general body of the faithful to take part in Spiritualistic practices because of the moral and physical dangers involved. The forces, often being far from spiritual, and sometimes malignant, are particularly disquieting and harmful to the idly curious and emotionally unstable people who are most attracted to the séance rooms. There is an ever present danger of obsession and possession by undesirable entities.

Nevertheless, "To genuine students who are well grounded in theological principles, and sufficiently versed in psychology to deal with these manifestations in a scientific spirit, permission may be accorded to experiment with a medium and attend séances."

Father Thurston himself, with the permission of the Church, carried out a good deal of controlled psychic research; he is well known, inside and outside the Church, as a serious, intelligent, unprejudiced investigator. Thurston was of the opinion, I have learned in conversation with Roman Catholic priests, that some of the phenomena in séance rooms, and all poltergeist activities, were the work of elementals. This is fairly well in line with Theosophical thought on the subject.

The *lamas* of Tibet give similar explanations and warnings. They were always strenuously opposed to spirit evocation as it is practiced in séances in the West, claiming that the entities thus contacted were more often than not "senseless ghosts, or psychic shells which have been cast off by the consciousness principle, and which, when coming into rapport with a human 'medium,' are galvanized into automaton-like life."* By "senseless ghosts" they probably mean the type of entity known to occultists as shades or specters.

The Tibetan *lamas* maintained that psychic research should be conducted only by masters of the occult

---

*See *The Tibetan Book of the Dead*, Oxford University Press, 1960 edition, page 187, Footnote 1.

sciences, and not indiscriminately by the ignorant and untrained populace.

The Rosicrucians, too, are against the practice of spirit communication as found in modern Spiritualism. There is, they say, a much better way of communicating.

When the soul enters the spiritual realm, it is able to make telepathic contact with all other souls in the universe, whether they are in or out of the physical body. The departed ones do not need to "come back to earth," so to speak, to hold intercourse with the living. Each individual soul has a conscious link with all others through the Oversoul. All are part of this One Universal Consciousness, and can make meaningful contact with each other through it.

But there is an obstacle to overcome when the intercourse is attempted between souls in the body and those out of the body. While a living man is in waking consciousness, he is normally out of touch with his own soul, or higher ego, which is the listening post and transmitting center for telepathic communications. Messages received at this listening post cannot usually be passed on to the waking consciousness because this is fully and intensely occupied with its daily stream of thoughts and feelings.

Perhaps something felt to be an impression, a hunch or an intuition may at times force its way through the barrier to waking consciousness. In the borderline state of consciousness — between sleep and waking — a more complete message may come through from the soul center. Then, again, the soul may use a dream to embody the message. If the dream is vivid and dramatic enough, the person on waking will remember it. Hopefully, it will be understood, but on the other hand the message may become distorted and confused through the mind's activity as it comes back to the waking state.

Yet, it is taught, telepathic communications between the souls of the living and the so-called dead go on constantly. Space, time and death create no barrier to this timeless, spaceless communion. The only barrier is the busy, self-centered mortal mind in the physical body. To converse telepathically with the spiritual realm the living must find a way through this barrier.

Rosicrucian teachings do not, however, approve of the mediumistic method of breaking the barrier, maintaining there is a danger of impostors, mischievous and even malignant entities, coming through the doorway opened by the medium. One method of penetration, well known to all occult teachings, is, of course, the regular and correct practice of *yoga* disciplines and meditation.

Although Swedenborg lived before the birth of modern Spiritualism, some of the things he said about communicating with spirits are of considerable interest in this context. While he himself had the rare gift of being able to visit the realms beyond death, to see and converse there without difficulty, he warns of the dangers of deception for the ordinary person. He gives some reasons for this.

Spirits have, he said, the extraordinary faculty of tapping a living person's memory and store of knowledge, whether it be in the sciences, languages or in any other subject. They enter into the person's mind, conjoin themselves with his thoughts and feelings, and in a moment come into possession of all that he has learned. Thus, from the person's own mind, which is an open book to them, the spirits converse with him.

It follows that, "with the learned they are learned; with the ingenious they are ingenious; with the prudent they are prudent; with the ignorant they are ignorant . . ." and so on.

The spirits, he said, do in fact have their own knowledge but, for various reasons, they are not permitted to use this when conversing with man. If spirits were to speak from their own memories and knowledge, it would cause the greatest confusion; therefore they leave their own spiritual state, enter into the living person's natural state and, merging with the person's mental life, speak from that as if it were their own.

It is not so much that they are deceivers as that they are themselves deceived, for, in putting on all things belonging to the living man, they become so identified with him that they believe his memory and knowledge are their own.

This is how Swedenborg regarded the case of spirit communication that apparently took place in his day, before the great flood of phenomena that came with the following century's Spiritualistic movement.

He made a further observation and warning: "Many persons believe that man might be taught by the Lord by means of spirits speaking with him; but those who believe this, and desire to do so, are not aware that it is connected with a danger to their souls."

Dr. Robert Crookall, the British scientist who over many years made a comparative study of a great wealth of spirit communications from many quarters, points out the limitations and dangers as well as the usefulness of such methods of investigation.

He says that probably ninety-nine per cent of the beings communicating from the unseen are still in the Hades conditions, by which he means that they are in the lower astral sub-planes near the earth. They are, therefore, often in a dreamy, lethargic state of consciousness. If they are newly dead, they repeat the opinions held during life. If they are long dead, but earthbound, they are usually ignorant, sometimes antisocial, and often boasters, jokers, liars and impostors.

Yet they can read thoughts and auras and, therefore, can talk about past events in the sitters' lives. Often, by keenly observing trends of thought and emotion, they can forecast future events — sometimes correctly, or nearly so. They may also have the power to produce apports, levitations, materializations and other physical phenomena. They may think and state that they are in the true spirit world, though they are in Hades.

Another source of deception and confusion is the fact that some communications are a result of telepathy from the living (medium or sitters), while still others are from astral shades who are able to read the memory traces of a sitter in his etheric body, or, as Crookall calls it, the "vehicle of vitality."

Although there are some wicked and malicious entities who at times succeed in coming through, Crookall found little or no evidence of non-human devils or demons. Even so, there is more than enough danger from "human" demons for the uninitiated who dabble in these matters.

But this dark and depressing side of spirit communication is not the whole picture according to this scientist. There are souls in the "Paradise" conditions of the higher astral regions who are able to communicate with people on earth. They may do this through what is called a mental medium. Generally speaking, however, there has to be a compromise: the medium has to raise his or her vibrational level and the spirit must lower its in order that they meet at a common point of intercourse. If it is necessary for the discarnate spirit to lower the vibration rate of consciousness much, it will become less alert and go more into the dreamy state. Then the spirit is liable to have memory lapses and transmit errors. When a sitter finds that a communicating spirit seems to have odd gaps in memory and thought, he should remember the clouding effects of near-earth conditions, and understand that the spirit is not able to be its true self.

Crookall claims, nevertheless, that there are some highly spiritual souls in the upper astral regions who can come through a very high type of medium without the necessity of greatly lowering the vibrations of his consciousness. In such cases very satisfactory messages are received. He gives as examples the discarnate father and sister of the investigator, Reverend C. Drayton Thomas; these often communicated with interesting results through the medium Mrs. Osborne Leonard.

When a soul has reached the heaven world, the vibrational gap between him and earth consciousness is too great for any direct mediumistic communication. If one from heaven gives a message in this way, it is done generally through a proxy in the astral plane. Likewise, if physical phenomena are planned by a spirit of either the heaven or upper astral planes, they must be carried out by an intermediary who is in the lower astral conditions.

This interesting idea of higher spirits using intermediaries or proxies in the lower regions to produce phenomena on earth was suggested long ago by the Shakers, a religious sect, experiencing spiritist phenomena several decades before the upsurge of modern Spiritualism.

Speaking of the fantastic materializations at the Eddy farmhouse in Vermont last century, Mr. Frederick Evans of the Shakers told Colonel H. S. Olcott that, though the materializations were carried out by spirits close to the earth, they were probably controlled by higher spirits. "They who *plan* the labor on a farm do not always *perform* the labor," he said.

On the subject of ghosts, Robert Crookall came to certain definite conclusions. They may be, he said, one of several different things: the double of a living person; the soul of a dead person; an astral shell or shade with little or no consciousness, or a thought-form created by someone either living or dead. The latter type of ghost, when seen by non-psychic people, has probably been materialized by the use of ectoplasm from a mediumistic person in the immediate vicinity.

When the ghost is a surviving soul delayed in the lower astral regions, it will, says Crookall, often make the request: "Pray for me!" This means that the departed soul is in very unhappy conditions and perhaps does not know why he is trapped there. It knows only that it needs help. The prayers of the living can certainly help the dead.

Men have talked with spirits for centuries, though in ancient times it was, on the whole, left to the priests of the temples. It seems, however, that there were some ex-temple magicians and witches who evoked the spirits. Though the Bible warns against such communication, King Saul himself once visited a witch (medium) at Endor to speak to the spirit of the prophet Samuel. This availed him little, but if Saul broke his own law against intercourse with the dead, no doubt scores of others were doing so.

But a hundred and thirty years ago, for some occult reason, the practice came out into the open, and spread like a raging fire through the dry spiritual wastelands of the West. Many, at the beginning, thought that Spiritualism would be the answer to man's eternal questions on the destiny of the soul. They thought it was the foundation of a new popular religion.

But it proved otherwise. The reason can be found, I think, in the analyses, judgements and warnings given by those who have taken the trouble and time to delve deeply into the phenomena.

Though the great occultists, seers and serious investigators have approached the subject from different individual angles, they are in agreement on certain fundamental conclusions. Communications cannot all be explained away by imputing great powers, even incredible powers, to the mind of the medium. There are independent intelligences communicating. A proportion of these may be non-human entities of some kind, but at least some are what they claim to be — souls of the departed — thus proving that the "dead" are still alive somewhere.

But, unfortunately, the voices of the dead prove little beyond survival. When the investigator has picked his way through the minefields of deception and pierced the thick screen of mist to hear the voice of a friend from the other side, what does he find? That "the dead know nothing," as the Bible says. Swedenborg and Crookall give good, if different, reasons for this. The communicating spirit is either in the semi-conscious Hades state, or has his consciousness dimmed and befogged by coming into the earth atmosphere, or — as Swedenborg sees it — the spirit unites himself so much with the mind of the living person that he gets all his ideas from there. Maybe all these factors play a part in lowering communications to a level where they teach little beyond the reality of life after death.

Besides the unreliability and inanity of most of the messages received, there is, the experts agree, a danger to people seeking contact with the dead. They may achieve a contact they did not desire, in the form, perhaps, of attaching spirits, or even possession by some earthbound evil entity.

Furthermore, apart from the risks run and the fact that the ordinary person gains little of value from constant attendance at spiritist séances, the practice in general is bad for those contacted on the other side. It stimulates and maintains their interest in affairs of the earth, and their attachments here. It thus tends to keep them near the earth for long periods when their interests should be turning to higher spiritual realms and they should be making progress in that direction. It is understandable that a person of no firm faith, when he has lost a loved one in death, has an urge to find out, in any way possible, if the loved one still lives somewhere. But if he has established this fact to his satisfaction through Spiritualism, he should leave it at that. He should not seek constant intercourse with the departed one through Spiritualist meetings, for this will hold back the loved one's spiritual progress, and do the seeker himself no good. He will gain no further knowledge or wisdom this way. He should remember that his life is here, and the life of the departed one is there — far beyond this vale of tears in the happier land of the spirit.

There are, nevertheless, some aspects of Spiritualism that seem to be positive and helpful. Rescue circles, such as that conducted by Air Marshal Lord Dowding in England during World War Two, appear to do a great deal of good. In war time, particularly, thousands of people are meeting with violent and sudden death. Dr. Robert Crookall concludes from his studies (as explained in Chapter Four) that such people are not usually met by friends, relatives or other kinds of helpers from the other side of death. Many problems, therefore, arise, particularly when there are mass deaths. The workers in rescue groups of the Spiritualistic movement try to make the bewildered deceased ones understand that they are really dead, and give them help and guidance until deliverers come from the other side to guide the souls into the undiscovered country.

Another aspect of Spiritualism that seems to have value is mediumistic healing of the sick. This is carried out in many countries today. It can be effected when the patient is either in the immediate presence of the medium, or many miles away.

The late Harry Edwards, probably the most famous in England, is reputed to have cured many people, both through direct personal contact and through absent healing. There are several other well known mediumistic healers now practicing in England, America and other countries. Most believe they know the names of the spirits who are working through them. Sometimes the name of a famous medical man, recently deceased, is given. Such a name creates faith, of course, and helps bring positive results. In fact, however, it may well be some other healing spirit using the famous name for therapeutic purposes.

Two countries where this branch of Spiritualism is very active are Brazil and the Philippines. Considerable research work by trained investigators has been done, particularly in the Philippines.

The mediumistic healers there have a Christian background, and most of them belong to a Spiritualist organization, members of which, I understand, give them certain training. They all began life as simple villagers, giving healing when required to the folk of their own community.

But then their fame spread to the western world and people from America, Europe and Australia began to arrive with chronic, apparently incurable, diseases, and pockets full of money. Accustomed to the high scale of payment for medical services in their countries, their donations to the healers were often munificent. Greed for gold, dreams of wealth and luxury led many of the simple psychic healers astray. In attempting to deal constantly with the large stream of wealthy patients, their psychic powers inevitably began to wane, and many started to cheat a little — or a lot, as required.

The result was that when the scientific investigators came on the scene, they found a confusing mixture of deception and genuine power, often in the same healer. But whether carried out by psychic power, sleight of hand, or a combination of both, the psychic surgery in particular was dramatic and almost incredible to sophisticated eyes.

On a visit to the Philippines I saw, as many have seen, the skin opened by waving a finger over it, a foot or more away. But I am also aware that the same healer uses a razor blade hidden in a swab of cotton wool to begin the opening when his power is weak. He probably sees nothing wrong with mixing some physical power with psychic power if the results are the same in faith and belief to bring about a healing. This man has effected many cures, but also has had many failures.

I went to see the work of one of the few healers who, in the experience of the investigators, never resorts to cheating. This was Josephine Sisson who operates in her simple home in the village of her birth. Permitted to stand close to her while she worked on patients, I saw her apparently press her fingers inside the skin, bringing out copious quantities of blood and other items, such as cysts and pieces of metal. The patients feel no pain at all while this is happening. Whatever opening she may make in the skin, closes and heals immediately, and there is no mark or scar left.

All the healers are in a state of trance while working, though this is hard to detect. It seems to be very different from the usual trance of the séance room, where the medium sits unconscious in a chair, with eyes closed. The healers I saw showed no outward signs of the trance state. Yet, in their "surgeries", I felt the same vibration, the same indescribable, somewhat dingy atmosphere, that I have experienced at many spiritist centers. With Josephine Sisson and Vergilio Guttierez, however, I felt a lighter, more spiritual vibration, which may mean that the spirits possessing them were of a higher type.

It is certain that these uneducated villagers, without any knowledge of anatomy, physiology or medical science could not do the things they do by their own skill. Even the percentage of *legerdemain* is probably carried out, when necessary, by whatever entities are working through them. Likewise the much publicized materialization or apport of animal or human tissue, from either outside or inside the patient, is far beyond the power of these simple folk in their normal state of consciousness. There are certainly, in my opinion, entities of another dimension working through these healers, as they themselves claim. But the type of entities using them will depend a good deal on the kind of lives they live. The purer, the less self-seeking the healer, the higher the level of spirits he will attract. Healers who have completely sold out to materialistic gain may do more harm than good to their patients.

But how much good do any of them actually do? The cases that come to them are usually those given up by orthodox medicine as hopeless. Yet there are cures in the Philippines and elsewhere where spiritist healing is practiced. I personally know of some dramatic ones. At the same time, many who go there come away no better in health, and poorer in wealth, than when they went. So much depends on the attitude of the patients themselves. Ultimately, whatever healing techniques are used, orthodox or otherwise, there is only Self-healing.

Investigators cannot say with authority what percentage of patients are cured in the Philippines. It is estimated by some that about two per cent are healed immediately, and a much larger percentage will find a cure coming about after a period of time — weeks or months or longer. But a large percentage just go home and die. Outwardly it seems to be a gamble, but actually it depends on many factors other than the power of the healers — factors such as *karma*, the strength of the subconscious desire to be healed and the level of faith in things unseen.

On the whole, however, psychic or mediumistic healing can be marked up as a plus for Spiritualism.

The interesting question remains: does any new knowledge ever come through a medium from entities existing in the dimensions beyond death? Though most of their communications are of a trite, unimportant nature, there are at times exceptions when stimulating discourses on philosophy and related subjects come through. But though stimulating and interesting, is there any of this material that cannot be found in the earthly writings of philosophers and sages?

A good example to study in this regard are the

communications coming through the medium Jane Roberts (herself a writer) from an entity known as Seth.

The main point of the philosophy he expounds and presents through many different verbal approaches is that consciousness creates form. It creates the whole physical universe, and every other universe of temporary reality in which we may have lived before birth, and may find ourselves in after death. Behind this and every other phenomenal universe there is one permanent unchanging Reality. The seemingly real physical world around us is a camouflage, created by consciousness through our senses, of the actual Reality. In like manner, the systems of reality we will experience after death are consciousness created, though based on the One Reality, which Seth calls 'All That Is.'

These philosophic ideas are, of course, found in Vedanta; they were given out long ago in the Upanishads by the ancient *rishis*, while similar concepts were later expressed by Plato. Seth, however, puts ancient wine into modern jars.

One idea he puts forward is, however, new, at least to me. Consciousness, he says, flutters and fluctuates; consequently its creation, the phenomenal universe, flickers on and off. The thought is that our bodies and all things around us are not constantly and continuously *there*. The gaps when they are not there are as long as the periods when they are. It is rather like the cinema where the gaps between the pictures are not perceived, and all appears to be flowing and continuous. This is an interesting idea and may be true.

Seth, who claims to have lived many lives on earth, remembering them all, has a few things to say about death and what comes after.

Consciousness, he says, may take a long or short time to withdraw from the body, depending on many variables. When it has, you may or may not realize that you are dead because you will be in a form that appears to you to be physical. When, however, you attempt to manipulate within the physical system, you will find, perhaps to your dismay and bewilderment, that there is a difference between what you were and what you are. There is, however, an order of personalities, which he calls an 'honorary guard,' who are ready to help you know what has happened, and to cross the border. This guard is made up of people who are dead and living (usually, out of their bodies). This is in agreement with Theosophical and other teachings.

Strong beliefs in experiences and places to be met with after death can cause you to hallucinate such places as, for example, the traditional heavens and hells, though such stereotyped existences are only temporary. It is better for happiness and progress not to have inflexible detailed mental pictures about the nature of after-death locales. Your ideas will certainly color your experiences, and you will interpret all experiences in the light of your strong beliefs.

The Review, or Judgement, about which we hear from the religious teachings and the researchers is, according to Seth, a self-review in which you examine the fabric of your last life, and learn to understand that your experiences were the results of your own thoughts and emotions. When you perceive the significance and meaning of your last life, you are ready to move on to a fuller understanding of your own soul, your own entity, of which your last personality on earth was but a facet. This is good Theosophy.

Further, in agreement with the different occult teachings, Seth says that the period between death and rebirth on earth varies greatly. It may be centuries, years, or only hours, depending on many different factors relating to the individual.

Seth makes a great deal of the validity of the human soul and its immortality. The portion, the personality, that you know as *you* is but one dimension of your multi-dimensional soul. But this one aspect cannot be erased or separated from the whole entity of which it is an integral part — as a facet of a cut diamond is part and parcel of the diamond. The part, united to the total individuality, continues to exist.

Seth echoes the ancient *rishis* when he says that the main purpose of life — the many lives we live — is to come to a full realization of our oneness with All That Is, which Vedanta calls *Brahman*.

On the question of communications between this world and the next, he says that messages through mediums can appear contradictory because the experiences of the dead are not the same. Conditions vary, situations vary, psychological states vary. An individual talking of the reality in which he finds himself can only explain what he knows. He probably knows nothing of the conditions of other realities that exist beyond his psychological state. Thus descriptions and explanations often vary a good deal, and this offends the human intellect that demands answers and descriptions that tally. This reinforces and confirms some of the ideas put forward by investigators into the occult, as explained earlier.

Even though, on the whole, the material given out by Seth is not new, the publication of it seems to me to have been well worthwhile. Not only does it lend renewed support to some basic concepts of Vedanta and the Ancient Wisdom generally, but it expresses the old verities in a unique, individualistic style, using modern phraseology and imagery. It should, therefore, help in re-establishing faith in the deeper truths of life, and spread them over a wider field.

Such unusual ventures in communications are no doubt of value, along with Spiritualistic healing, rescue work and serious psychic research by qualified people. But unless one is engaged in some positive and worthwhile aspect of Spiritualism, one would be wise to follow the advice of the experts and leave this unpredictable, unprofitable, sometimes dangerous practice of conversing with "spirits" alone.

No birth, no death, no caste have I,
Father, mother, have I none.
I am He, I am He, Blessed Spirit,
I am He.

Adi Shankara

7

There Is No Death

The Search of Nachiketas

The Katha Upanishad tells the story of a boy's search for the meaning of death, a search so intense and earnest that it took him right to the abode of the Hindu god of death, Lord Yama.

The story began at a great ritual sacrifice in the India of ancient Vedic times. This sacrifice symbolizes the spiritual truth that, through the renunciation of possessions, through the dedication of all worldly wealth to God, man reaches happiness and eternal life. Long after Vedic days Christ taught this same great truth, and illustrated it in his life. In modern times, Tenko-san of Japan taught and lived by the same exacting principle.

But for the ordinary human being it is by no means an easy sacrifice to make. And Vajasrava, who was performing the ritual in our Vedic story, was more human than God-like. Nachiketas, his son, who was watching, soon observed that the ceremony was falling far short of the ideal. His father was offering to the gods cows too old to give milk, cattle too weak to eat grass or drink water. In fact, in a pretense of sacrificial offering, the father was simply getting rid of his useless stock.

"What hypocrisy!" thought the boy. "Even if my father is not willing to give all his wealth, surely he should give something he really values to God. Otherwise there is no sacrifice. This hollow pretense must bring him sorrow rather than happiness."

Knowing that his father loved him very much, Nachiketas asked: "To whom will you sacrifice me, Father?" Vajasrava was silent. Nachiketas asked again and was again answered with silence. When he asked a third time, the father grew angry and replied: "I will give you to Yama, God of Death."

Later, when Vajasrava calmed down, he felt very sorry, but the words were spoken, and Nachiketas was intent on going to see Yama. "The pursuit of truth is the gateway to the abode of the Eternal," he reminded his father. That pursuit was dearer to him than love of father, dearer than life itself. Fearlessly he left home to seek the abode of Yama.

But, reaching there, he found that Yama was not at home. For three days and nights he waited, without food or drink, determined at all cost to find the truth. At the end of this period Yama returned, and was very contrite to find that a guest had received such a poor welcome at his home.

Yama said: "Since you have come as a sacred guest, and have had no hospitality for three days, I will grant you three boons of your own choice."

Nachiketas' first request concerned his father. He asked that when he returned, Vajasrava would welcome him home with forgiveness and love. Yama granted this boon, adding, "When he sees you free from the jaws of death, sweet will be his sleep at night."

This dialogue indicates that Nachiketas did not, in fact, die in order to attain communion with the God of Death; he perhaps went through what today would be called a near-death experience.

For his second boon Nachiketas asked about the way of attaining heaven after death. He said: "There is no fear in heaven: old age and death are not there. The good rejoice there, beyond hunger and thirst and sorrow. You know, O Yama, the sacrifice, the sacred fire that leads to heaven. Explain it to me since I have faith."

Yama was quite happy to grant this favor. "The sacred fire which is the means of attaining the infinite worlds, and is also their foundation," he said, "is hidden in the sacred place of the heart." He went on to describe the ritual of the fire sacrifice which, if correctly performed, takes man at death beyond sorrow into the regions of heaven.

But this was not sufficient for Nachiketas. He knew there was something more, and he was determined to seek for the root of the mystery of life and death. All things compounded must come to an end, so heaven, like earth, must pass away in the fullness of time. But what about eternity? Did man have an eternal spirit, beyond time, without beginning, without end? Some say he has; some say he has not. What was the truth of the matter? The answer to this question was the third boon he asked of Yama.

Now, for the first time, the God of Death hesitated. "Even the gods in times of old had doubts about this mystery," he said. "Kindly release me from this boon and ask another."

Nachiketas replied: "What greater teacher could I find to explain the mystery than the King of Death himself? There is no other boon so great as this."

Then Yama tempted Nachiketas to take instead all the treasures that earth can provide, even to dominion over the vast earth itself.

But Nachiketas, like Christ, was not to be tempted

in this way. "All these earthly pleasures pass away,"
he said. "Indeed, how short is life: when a mortal
here on earth has sensed his own immortality, could
he wish for a life of pleasure, of lust for deceitful
beauty and wealth? No! Grant me the promised
boon. Unveil the mystery of the great beyond. This
is the only gift Nachiketas can ask."

Thus, held firmly to his promise, and realizing that
the boy was in earnest and worthy of the sacred
knowledge, Lord Yama began to expound.

What he expounded forms the essence of the great
spiritual philosophy of Vedanta.

Vedantic Window on Life and Death

The Upanishads, coming at the end of the Vedas
as commentaries and interpretations, were meant for
serious, worthy searchers after Truth, typified by
Nachiketas. Though the Katha Upanishad contains a
more unified exposition of the Vedantic concepts
than any other, most of the Upanishads contribute
something to the philosophy.

The teachings contained in them were later system-
atized into a work known as the Brahma Sutras or
the Vedanta Sutras. These *sutras*, being brief apho-
risms, themselves require expansion and explanation
and, through the centuries, there have been many
commentaries by great sages.

Three leading commentators since the beginning
of the Christian Era were Adi Shankara, Ramanuja
and Madhava. Though drawing the same conclusions
on basic issues, these eminent sages differ on a number of metaphysical points. Consequently, their three
commentaries have brought about three schools of
Vedanta philosophy. These are known as Advaita,
Visishtadvaita, and Dvaita Vedanta, or, in English,
non-dualism, qualified non-dualism and dualism.

Since these differing interpretations concern, among other things, the ultimate fate of the human soul, they are part of our subject here.

Let us first look at the points on which the three great commentators agree and which, therefore, form the main pillars of the broad, noble edifice of Vedanta.

The first pillar is that behind, and at the same time within, the phenomenal universe is an eternal Reality that cannot be perceived by our five senses or cognized by our reasoning minds. Vedantists call this Absolute Eternal Reality *Brahman.*

Another pillar is that, though *Brahman* exists within and beyond everything, the easiest place to find It is within ourselves. When we find It there, we find It everywhere, and we know that we are one with It. This knowledge, coming as a great experience of identity with the Divine, removes the fundamental ignorance in which we live. Then we are liberated from the bonds in which we have bound ourselves through the ignorance of our true identity.

This key to the nature of man, discovered by the mystics for themselves, and taught in ancient times only to those disciples deserving of the privilege of sitting at the feet of the Master, is now being taught to the multitudes by Sri Satya Sai Baba, as well as other teachers. He is not only spreading wide the doctrine that all are one with God, but teaching the life to be lived, and the spiritual exercises to be practiced, in order to reach the great liberation. If enough can understand and achieve this, the world will be changed, and a new era of enlightenment and peace will begin.

Another pillar of Vedanta is that *Brahman* is the cause of the universe, though how it caused It to be is a point on which the commentators do not agree.

To come closer to our main theme of death and what comes after, the teachings of Vedanta on this are close to those of Theosophy and other esoteric doctrines. Though details differ, there is fundamental agreement on general lines.

Vedanta is not, however, very expansive about the after-death planes of existence, being more concerned with the illumination and liberation that will take us beyond the planes. It does, however, have something to say on the subject, and also on the necessity of reincarnation for the vast numbers who have not yet reached God-realization and freedom from the round of births and deaths.

The Hindu Puranas give much more detail about the planes, locales and *post mortem* conditions of the unliberated souls. So from the Upanishads and Puranas together we can form a fairly complete picture of Hindu ideas on the fate of the human soul after death.

Though there are many places called *lokas*, all of them seem to be classified under a few main planes. There is Bhuvarloka which corresponds roughly with the Theosophical astral plane. It interpenetrates the earth plane, Hinduism teaches, and extends for some distance beyond it. Then there is the mental plane, which they call Svargaloka. This interpenetrates the astral, but extends further into space than does the latter. Beyond the mental plane (Svarga) are four other worlds belonging to the higher evolution of the soul. These are called Maharloka, Janaloka, Tapoloka and Satyaloka. All seven worlds — from the earth (Bhuloka) to Satyaloka — are contained in the Cosmic Egg, within which the creative work of Brahma proceeds. But, according to the Vishnu Purana, two other regions lie beyond the Egg, yet can be reached from it. These are called Vaikuntha and Goloka.

Each *loka*, as a state of existence, represents a form of the Divine Consciousness, and a modification of matter expressing that state of consciousness. As the individual soul is of the nature of God, it is capable of realizing these seven states of consciousness, and therefore of living in any of the seven worlds, through appropriate changes of individual consciousness.

The first three *lokas*, the earth, the astral and the heaven regions, are those in which the soul lives during its long evolution on the wheel of births and deaths. They are known as the three worlds, or Tri-loka. The higher *lokas* — corresponding approximately to the causal plane of Theosophy — are not reached by the soul till it is very highly evolved. All the regions within the Cosmic Egg are destroyed at the time of the dissolution of the universe, but the two regions beyond, Vaikuntha and Goloka, are said to be everlasting.

There are also seven regions of matter grosser than the earth. These are called *talas* and are various types of hells, to which evil persons may go. In these the individual will suffer to expiate his wrong-doing before returning to earth for another incarnation, another attempt to poise his life at last, and learn to be true to his own deeply buried Self, "being one with which we are one with the whole world."*

Furthermore, many places exist within the main seven *lokas* that stretch from earth upward to Satya-loka, near the shell of the Cosmic Egg. These places are all named in the Hindu scriptures. At the lower levels, yet above the *talas*, is, for example, Pretaloka, where the soul still feels strong sensual cravings and earthly desires. The miseries and torments here can

---

*See *Empedocles on Etna* by Matthew Arnold.

be very intense indeed. But in time, helped by the prayers of loved ones on earth, the soul is able to break from the prison of desire and worldly attachments and move to higher and happier levels.

One of the regions on a higher level is Pitriloka, the place where the *pitris*, or forefathers, dwell. People who on earth have lived good, but not truly spiritual, lives (in other words, average citizens) may go to this place. There they live happily with their ancestors for long periods, after which they may reincarnate on earth.

Lord Krishna, in the Bhagavad-Gita, said, "Those who worship the ancestors will go to the ancestors." And it is to Pitriloka that they go.

But within the heaven worlds there are higher states of happiness than found in Pitriloka. Those who worship the gods will go to the gods, said Krishna, and there are many splendid abodes of the lesser gods to which people may go — Indraloka, Varunaloka, Kuberaloka and others.

The life and conditions in all *lokas* are described in various Hindu Puranas. They are all celestial abodes where, among the shining ones, the *devas*, virtuous souls may live long periods in great felicity. In radiant, beautiful bodies, they will have great powers over, and freedom within, the subtle matter of their worlds.

Heaven, where souls reap the happy rewards of their good actions, where there is no conflict, and wishes always come true, is a place where felicitous, unalloyed happiness is experienced. There being no struggle, no resistance, the soul does not develop the strength to break through the shell and reach eternal union with God. It seems to need the solid springboard of life on earth in order to reach the very highest level of its destiny.

When it finally breaks through the Cosmic Egg into the supernal regions beyond, the soul may remain there, within the inner courts of the true Spiritual Home, until the end of the cycle when it will merge into the Godhead. On the other hand, some advanced souls will merge with the Divine, and attain complete liberation from bondage, immediately after leaving their physical bodies.

To sum up the Hindu teachings about life after death, and put them in simple terms: there are seven regions, including the earth, that extend upward in subtler matter and higher states of consciousness. Within these, like countries in a continent, there are many particular locations to which a soul may go, for varying periods, according to its development and special interests.

There are also seven regions going downwards, from the earth level, through grosser, coarser matter and lower states of consciousness with appropriate suffering for evil deeds done.

Whether the soul's actions on earth take it to higher or lower levels of existence, it will return eventually to earth for another life and another opportunity to attain perfection.

The soul's evolution on the wheel of births and deaths takes place within the enclosing ring of creation, known as the Cosmic Egg. Beyond the ring lie the Divine, uncreate, eternal regions where the soul returns to its true home in God.

For those who awaken to this deeper understanding and realize their identity with God, while still living a human life on earth, there is no death. There is only the concept of casting aside the physical sheath, like a piece of packaging that has served its purpose and is needed no more.

But what really is this state of emancipation and

union with the Divine? The great commentators on the Vedanta Sutras do not themselves agree about the nature of God and the ultimate destiny of the human soul.

Adi Shankara holds that *Brahman* is without attributes. That is, we cannot attribute any finite, limiting qualities to *Brahman*. We can only say It is *Satchitananda* — absolute existence, absolute consciousness and infinite bliss. Other commentators draw a different conclusion from the Sutras, and see *Brahman* as a personal God with infinite benign attributes.

To Shankara, the non-dualist, the *advaitist*, there is naught but *Brahman*, the One without a second. The universe does not really exist. It has an apparent existence to man because his mortal mind and senses perceive something that is not really there — just as we see a mirage in the desert, or imagine that we see a snake when we see only a rope. Our minds have superimposed the non-existent mirage of water and palm trees on the desert, or the image of a snake on the percept of a rope.

In the same way we, through our senses, superimpose this manifold universe on the One Existence which is *Brahman*. So the universe has only a mental existence. It is like a passing magic lantern show; the permanent "screen" behind it being the One Existence.

But other commentators say that this doctrine is wrong, that the universe, though constantly changing, is real. It is produced by *Brahman* and is, indeed, a mode or expression of *Brahman* Itself.

The differing opinions within Vedanta apply to the ultimate fate of the human soul. To Shankara, the individual separate soul has no existence. Our belief in it is part of the illusion. Only *Brahman* exists, and we are identical with *Brahman* — as the space in an earthen pot is identical with the infinite space outside it — which is demonstrated when the pot is broken. Likewise, when the illusory shell that divides us from *Brahman* is broken, we realize that we are one with the One Life; we realize that there are not the many individual selves, but just the One Self.

So, the ultimate fate of the individual soul is to merge completely in *Brahman*, as the "dewdrop slips into the shining sea." *Brahman* being beyond our human understanding, we cannot really understand this merged state of the human soul. The Buddhists call it *nirvana*, and Sir Edwin Arnold has the Buddha say, in *The Light of Asia*:

> If any teach Nirvana is to cease,
> Say unto such they lie.
> If any teach Nirvana is to live,
> Say unto such they err; not knowing this,
> Nor what light shines beyond their
>   broken lamps,
> Nor lifeless, timeless bliss.

So, no last word can be said about this state, if such state there be. But a question can be asked. If the individual ceases entirely to be, what was the purpose of his long evolutionary struggle towards the development of spiritual perfection in individual character? The answer to this metaphysical question we must, however, leave to eternity.

According to Ramanuja's interpretation, known as qualified non-dualism, individual souls have existed eternally as a mode of *Brahman*. They are not identical with *Brahman* but are a part of It. At the time of creation they are sent forth and, at the end of the cycle, they return into union with *Brahman*. This union does not seem to be the same as the complete mergence of Advaita Vedanta; while the emphasis is on union, some degree of individuality remains. It is more like the Theosophical concept of the evolved individual souls becoming close companions of God, co-workers in the divine plan.

Madhava, another leading commentator on the Brahma Sutras, teaches the Dvaita, or dualist, philosophy. He regards *Brahman* and the individual souls as independent entities, existing as such from and to eternity. There is no mergence, no union. *Brahman* is the ruler of the individual souls, as He is of the universe He creates, dissolves, then creates again — periodically through eternity.

Whatever is the ultimate truth about these various viewpoints of the great interpreters, the basic essence of Vedanta is that *Brahman*, the Sole Reality, has existed from, and will exist throughout, eternity — without beginning, without end. The universe, whatever degree of reality it may have, was caused by *Brahman*, or it is Its or His vesture, or "becoming mode."

The human soul, whether identical with *Brahman*, a part of It, or independent, likewise has eternal existence. The way out of the sorrows and conflicts, the ups and downs of human existence, into a state of beatitude is a direct knowledge of the Supreme God. This knowledge cannot be gained by reasoning or the outward turned senses, but only by turning inward to the source of all Being.

The essence of the Vedantic message given to Nachiketas by the God of Death is that there is no death for the one who can rise above it, and see the event in its true perspective, outside of time in the matrix of eternity.

Today many people from all countries are being instructed in these great truths by teachers like Satya Sai Baba, who teaches not only the perennial philosophy, but also the *yogic* practice for reaching Divine Union.

Where East Meets West — Christian Science

Born in America in the last quarter of the nine- teenth century, Christian Science bears some marked resemblances to Vedanta. There are historians of Christian Science who think that it is, to a large degree, the fruit of eastern influences that came to bear on the mind of its founder, Mrs. Mary Baker Eddy. Indeed, one occult school states that the behind the scenes initiator of the movement was an eastern master of the Great White Brotherhood.

But whether that be so, or whether the doctrines Mrs. Eddy expounds came to her as an inner reve- lation, as most of her followers claim, the spiritual concepts have the sweeping breadth of Vedanta, albeit colored by the author's Christian conditioning.

Speaking personally, I was introduced to Christian Science while still young, but could not understand it, nor grasp the great philosophical concepts behind it, until many years later, after I had studied Vedanta in India. For me Vedanta threw light on Christian Science and made its profound spiritual ideas acceptable.

Unfortunately its name, "Christian Science," nar- rows its public image, limiting its immediate interest to those of Christian upbringing. "Divine Science" would perhaps have been a better name, and Mrs. Eddy herself does sometimes use both this and "Spir- itual Science" interchangeably with "Christian Science."

She also points out that the Christ concept is not confined to the Christian era, but is without begin- ning and without end. The great spiritual truth, with its healing power, taught and embodied by Jesus

Christ at the beginning of the Age of Pisces, is as old as "the Ancient of Days." But this idea is not generally known and accepted, so it does not, therefore, overcome the limiting influence of the name.

But let us try to examine the points of agreement and disagreement between Vedanta and Christian Science on the questions of God, the universe, the nature of man and the meaning of his death.

God, Mrs. Eddy teaches, is One and All. There is no other existence apart from God, the Spirit, who fills all space.

The universe is not as we see it. Through our deceiving corporeal senses and mortal minds we perceive something that is not there at all — which we call the physical universe. We make the fundamental error of imposing an imaginary material universe on the true spiritual one, the Reality that is actually there, and is identical with God.

Man likewise is spiritual and one with God. What we call the physical body is an illusion and has no true existence. Individuals are the eternal reflections of God. As such, spiritual man has existed always and will exist forever. But individuals are not separate from God any more than the myriad reflections of the sun in the pools of water and rivers are separate from the sun. So far, Mrs. Eddy is pretty much in line with the ideas of Adi Shankara.

When she defines man as the image of God and coexistent with Him she is speaking of the true spiritual man — not as he will be in some future state, but as he is here and now, as he would see himself if he could but see truly with the spiritual senses. The true man is really divine mind, she says. He has no mind separate from God. He "possesses no life, intelligence nor creative power of his own, but reflects spiritually all that belongs to his Maker." He is wholly a reflection.

Like the eastern sages, Mrs. Eddy uses the simile of the dream to describe existence here. "Mortal existence is a dream of pain and pleasure in matter, a dream of sin, sickness and death." When we wake from a dream we have had while asleep, we feel that it was all just a state of the mind, with no reality. Mortal existence is the same: a dream sequence created from mental images. In both cases we think at the times of dreaming that our bodies and environments are real; in both cases we are wrong, for they are only mental projections.

Death is part of the mortal dream of life. Dreaming that he lives, man dreams that he dies. If, however, he is able to cast off the veil of error before his death, and perceive that he is, in fact, an immortal, spiritual being, he will know that there is in reality no death, as there was no birth. Both are just events in the mortal dream.

But if he does not have that great awakening to truth, which the Vedantins call the "knowledge of *Brahman*," he will go through the sad scenario of the mortal death and, passing beyond it, go into another waking dream. He will appear to himself just the same as before death, with a solid body, in solid material surroundings, almost identical to those he left behind. It will not seem at all like a dream. To the mortal who died, and who is still a mortal in another setting, it will all appear quite real. Dreams always do.

About the actual transition called "death," Mrs. Eddy says: "In the vestibule through which we pass from one dream to another, or when we awake from earth's sleep to the grand verities of Life, the departing may hear the glad welcome of those who have gone before." That welcome, that vision, may come, according to this statement, both to those who are passing from one dream to another, and also to those who are waking to the great truth of real existence.

The human mind, not liberated from the illusory belief in material existence, and still believing in the reality of a material body, will find itself after the transition with a "body like the one it had before death."

Such bodies, though quite real to the "dead," are unseen to those who bury the old discarded physical body, often thinking, sadly, that they are disposing of the one they had loved for a few short years, and now have lost forever.

But the real person is not lost, not dead; in fact, he cannot die. Beyond the veil he still carries on, either awake to true spiritual existence, or else in another dream life on another plane of existence. Mrs. Eddy does not have much to say about these intermediary planes. But the little she does say agrees in the main with the occult teachings.

About heaven and hell she expresses somewhat the same idea as Swedenborg when he said that, not God, but man casts himself into hell. Mrs. Eddy believed that sin is its own punishment and if that punishment has not been sufficient to reform a person while on earth, then "the good man's heaven would be a hell to the sinner. They who know not purity and affection by experience, can never find bliss in the blessed company of Truth and Love simply through transition into another sphere. Divine Science reveals the necessity of sufficient suffering, either before or after death, to quench the love of sin."

But whatever plane of existence the individual is on in the hereafter, whether it be the heaven of the good man, the hell of the sinner, or somewhere in

between, he will have to go through another transition, or "death," in order to awake from the mortal
dream into a realization of his true spiritual identity.
She writes: "Death will occur on the next plane of
existence as on this, until the spiritual understanding
of life is reached."

While in its doctrine that God is All, and that there
is nothing whatever apart from God, Christian Science is totally in agreement with Advaita Vedanta,
in other respects it is more akin to some of the other
schools of Vedanta.

The ultimate destiny of the individual after he
comes to an understanding of his spiritual reality and
identity with God, is not, according to Christian Science, what Adi Shankara taught. That is, individuals
do not merge with the formless Divine as a drop of
water merges with the ocean. On the contrary, they
remain unique individuals eternally.

But, no longer steeped in ignorance and error, no
longer deluded in the mortal sleep of prisoners, they
will know themselves to be individual reflections of
the One Existence, the One without a second. Aware
that each is a unique reflection of God, knowing the
truth of multiplicity in oneness, the individuals will
exist forever in understanding, peace and bliss.

This concept seems to lie somewhere between the
dualistic and qualified non-dualistic branches of
Vedanta. Yet it cannot really be identified with either.
It has overtones and nuances of its own, born, no
doubt, from its Christian background. Moreover,
Mrs. Eddy, with her western religious training, does
not bring in the reincarnation doctrine of Vedanta.

Even so, at the deepest conceptual levels, the
agreement between Vedanta and this Christian
denomination is amazing. If Mrs. Eddy was not influenced directly by an eastern teacher, nor by Vedantic

literature, she reached independently the same profound spiritual verities as expressed by the ancient *rishis,* the fathers of Vedanta.

It matters little that statements of ultimate truth vary to some degree. The deepest truth lies beyond words and, once expressed, is no longer entirely true. Both Vedanta and Christian Science are attempts to express the inexpressible; both seem to lie very close to Eternal Truth.

Mrs. Eddy and her followers have to a large degree demonstrated their understanding of Reality by their healing work. We all, while here, have to go along with the illusions of physical existence, knowing that they are not real in the true sense. But we do not have to accept the illusions of disharmony and disease. Those who practice Christian Science have demonstrated that disease can be banished by mentally refusing to accept even its temporary existence.

In the end, all Christian Scientists have to go through the illusion of physical death, of course, but they know it for what it is.

The Tibetan Book of the Dead

The profound understanding of the meaning of death found in Vedanta and Christian Science is encountered again in *The Tibetan Book of the Dead.* As with the other two, its presentation is closely interwoven with the cultural background of the people and place of its birth. Yet, in essence, the message is the same: there is no death for the individual who has come to a realization of the meaning of life. The Tibetans, however, add something more: they show how one might reach that realization at the time of death, and so escape the round of births and deaths.

The Tibetan title of the work, *Bardo Thodöl,* meaning "Liberation by Hearing on the After-Death

Plane," indicates the main purpose of the text, and the method of its use. It is read aloud to one who is dying, and the reading continues for some time after the person is dead. It offers a guide through the immediate after-death plane, telling the soul how to avoid the snares met with there, and find its way to the highest. The old Tibetans who composed the text and initiated the custom knew that the soul hears what is said during death and for some time afterwards, while it is still on the plane near the earth. *Bardo* is the place where the soul goes immediately after death, probably corresponding with one of the lower astral planes of Theosophy.

As for many generations the text was passed down orally from guru to guru, no one knows how long ago the *Bardo Thodöl* first came into being. But scholars consider that the text was first committed to writing in the eighth century A.D., in the time of the great founder of Lamaism, Padma Sambhava. The script was then hidden away for a long period. It was a "hidden" or "closed" book, known only to initiates who could understand it. But finally it was given to the public, and then came to the western world through a young Oxford graduate, Dr. T. W. Evans-Wentz. It was in the year 1919 that Evans-Wentz procured a copy of the manuscript from a *lama* attached to a monastery in Darjeeling. As soon as possible he had it translated into English by a great Tibetan scholar, Lama Kazi Dawa-Samdup.*

Dr. Evans-Wentz assisted the *lama* in turning the difficult Tibetan *tantric* text into idiomatic English,

---

*Lama Kazi Dawa-Samdup had been an interpreter for the British Government in Bhutan. Then he became a lecturer in Tibetan at the University of Calcutta which published his English-Tibetan Dictionary.

edited the work, and wrote a long, explanatory and profoundly interesting introduction. The book was published by the Oxford University Press in England in 1927.

For a later edition, Dr. Carl Jung wrote an appreciative "Psychological Commentary," stating that the book had been his constant companion since it was first published, and that he owed to it many fundamental insights. Praising it as the highest spiritual effort on behalf of the departed, he says that "every serious minded reader must ask himself whether these wise old *lamas* might not, after all, have caught a glimpse of the fourth dimension and twitched the veil from the greatest of life's secrets."

Jung says that while it was once a "closed" book and is now an "open" book — that is, all who wish to may read it — it is still in effect a "closed" book. Only those who have reached a certain spiritual understanding will be able to come to grips with its meaning. To the mass of mankind it will be simply bewildering and without meaning. Being able to read a book does not necessarily make it "open."

I myself first attempted to read *The Tibetan Book of the Dead* when I was a student at the Theosophical Headquarters in India, studying the Wisdom Teachings. It was too abstruse, perhaps, too symbolic for me at that time. I put it aside for later study. Again, it was Vedanta that gave me the key to the Tibetan book's fundamental teaching.

But first let us look at the practical side — the way in which some versions of the text (for there are several) have been used for untold generations in the land of mystery and mysticism.

When signs show that the soul is about to leave the body, the text is read or chanted aloud in the presence of the dying person. Then the reading continues in the presence of the corpse, and for some days after the funeral, while the soul is thought to be still within hearing of the spot where it left the body. There may be one or several *lamas* chanting the text, and the chanting may go on for fourteen days, or twenty-one, or even up to forty-nine days after the funeral. The number of days is always a multiple of the sacred seven.

The Tibetan Book of the Dead is, in one sense, a *requiem* prayer for the departed soul, but its aim is to take the soul beyond all heaven worlds into the liberated state of *nirvana*. Actually, the best time to study the book, which Evans-Wentz calls "an epitomized exposition of the cardinal doctrines of the Mahayana School of Buddhism," is during life. If an individual has done this, the hearing of it at the critical hour of death, during the changing state of consciousness, should act as a reminder of the teachings, and as a guide.

The length of the time in Bardo, within earshot of earth, so to speak, is variable and depends on the spiritual development of the departed soul. An advanced *yogi*, for instance, may experience Bardo for only a few minutes, and then pass on to whatever high state he is destined for. On the other hand, earthbound souls may be trapped in this region for very long periods.

According to the teachings in this book the newly dead person will, for a time, be the sole spectator of a series of vivid scenes. These, though seeming quite real, are a kind of private dream, resulting from the spectator's own consciousness-content. The scenes are at first very pleasant, then, after a period, quite horrible. But whether enticing or terrible, they are a trap. They will lead or drive the spectator into one of the phenomenal worlds which he must strive hard to avoid.

The Book of the Dead tells the discarnate individual how he should react to each scene. It keeps assuring him that the things he is seeing are merely images from his own consciousness, that they have no reality. The voice of the *lama* keeps imploring the soul to concentrate on the Light, the "Clear Light of the Void" that shines beyond the scenes. The Light is the Reality. By concentrating on it, and shunning all else, he will reach liberation. In fact, the time of death, bringing a greatly altered state of consciousness, is a person's wonderful opportunity. It is easier to reach emancipation, the spiritual goal, at this time than at any other. But the soul must do as instructed, or it will soon be lost again in the phenomenal worlds.

People who read *The Tibetan Book of the Dead* should not think that all who die must necessarily witness exactly the same scenario as described there. Such visualizations come from a Tibetan consciousness-content. As a person's mind is conditioned, as he has thought and felt and believed during life, so will his immediate after-death images be.

Found among the posthumous papers of Alexandra David-Neel, the French orientalist who spent many years in Tibet and wrote on the *yoga* and mysticism of that country, is an interesting dialogue between the Dalai Lama and herself. Part of it concerns this subject of the Bardo and what is witnessed there.

"Do Christians, though they follow the religion of Issu [Jesus], also go to Bardo when they die?" she asked.

"Certainly."

"But they don't believe in the gods of Lamaism, or in reincarnation, or in anything written in the *Bardo Thodöl*."

"They will still go to Bardo. However, what they see there will be Issu, angels, paradise, hell, and the like. In their projecting spirit they will see all the things they have been taught, and which they believe in. They will have visions which in some cases will frighten them, for instance, the Last Judgement and the torments of hell. Their images and experiences during their dream journey will be different from a Tibetan's. But in essence it will be the same thing. The psychomental impressions stored up during the individual's lifetime will take on forms and be represented as ensouled images. Thus the Tibetan, the Christian, or any other disembodied being will tend to view these visions as real events."

The images in an individual's visualizations depend, therefore, to a large degree on group culture, and to some degree on the way he reacted to that culture during life.

Also, the scenario is similar to what the researchers found in near-death experiences, where events of the past life pass before the eyes of the patient. In the case of the Bardo visions, however, instead of events it is a dramatized presentation of the person's mental and emotional life.

The Tibetan teachings show that the important thing is how the soul views these after-death scenes and its reaction to them. He is looking at thought-images of his past life, and he must make a great effort to rise above them into the higher realm. The text goes into great detail about this, and makes every effort to help the soul at this moment of truth.

The first thing it tells him is that at the time of transition he will see the Clear Light of the Void. This divine light is the source of all the lesser lights of sun, moon and stars. As it is so radiant and powerful the soul may be overawed by it and turn away. Furthermore, the propensities and interests he takes with him from the world may draw him away from such spiritual purity. He may feel that it is foreign to his nature.

If, on the other hand, during his life he has had sufficient spiritual training, he will understand that the radiant light is the Divine Reality. Then at this vital juncture, recognizing the light for what it is, he must strive to become one with it, and take the "Great Straight Upward Path." Thus he will reach liberation without ever entering the Bardo plane.

The old Tibetan *yogis* who composed the book knew full well that only very rare souls would be able to merge with the Divine immediately after death. They, therefore, designed the text to help the individual progressively throughout the events of the Bardo dream. They advise him, for instance, to remember and repeat whatever devotional practices he knew during life. They beseech him above all to feel love and compassion in the heart. They keep telling him that he himself is in reality part of the light, and not of the phenomenal worlds. "Thine own consciousness, shining void and inseparable from the Great Body of Radiance, hath no birth nor death, and is the Immutable Light."

It is explained to the confused soul that the voidness he feels, and may be afraid of, is not the voidness of nothingness. Though empty of phenomena, it is in reality a fullness. It is the Primal Cause of all things.

Some people do not need to wait for the moment of death to see the divine light, but have a glimpse of it during their lives. It is, they say, "out of time," both "clear" and "white," more radiant and brilliant than the sun, suffused with bliss, love and peace.

Most who have had a near-death experience, and returned to tell the tale, have seen and felt the formless, yet somehow personified, benign light. With a friend of mine, however, the emphasis was more on the aspect of voidness. Describing it, or attempting to describe it, he said, "It was as though I was watching life itself — from the inside. There was no form; it was quite beyond time. In a way I seemed like a molecule in a great ocean. I can only say there was no emptiness; it was a 'full void.' It was teeming, vibrant life."

Through lack of understanding and spiritual training the soul is almost certain to be diverted from this Many Splendored Thing, and become attracted to its immediate surroundings, which at first are earthly. Near at hand he sees his relatives and friends, sad-eyed, mournful, weeping. Yet as he still has a body (the astral body), he feels confused. He speaks to his friends in the room, but they do not seem to hear and do not answer. Nevertheless, he can hear what they are saying to each other, and can also hear the voice of the *lama* chanting the *Bardo Thödöl*. If he pays attention, he will find that this voice is directing him, telling him, perhaps, that he must now meditate on the God he has worshipped in life, for that is his guardian God. He must not be distracted by anything around him. One-pointed concentration on his personal God and prayer are essential for his liberation now.

If ever during his life he has had a glimpse of spiritual truth, the voice tells him, he should now recognize that he is experiencing that truth fully. It is very urgent that he understands this while he is still in a state of mental equilibrium. Soon this balanced state will change, and the contents of his subconscious mind will be projected in overpowering visualizations. This will make his task more difficult. So now he must keep all his attention fixed on the light, and move towards it.

For the many who do not follow the instructions at this early stage, the *karmic* illusions — the dream pictures — soon begin to shine. At first they consist of what the Tibetans call the "peaceful deities." These come, it is said, from the individual's heart center, from his center of love, affection and related emotions. They are beautiful, colorful, happy dream images and, of course, seem quite real to the dreamer.

There is no point in describing in detail the Tibetan Bardo images, for they will have no significance to people of other cultures. The student may, if he desires, study them for himself in *The Tibetan Book of the Dead*.

But, whatever the images that come to any human being in the immediate *post mortem* state, the important thing to remember, the Tibetan *lamas* tell us, is that they are nothing more than a dream. The only Reality is the Light that shines behind and through the various scenes of the dream.

As the drama progresses, however, the clear light may assume different colors: blue, white, yellow, green, or red. But, whatever the color, it will always be radiant and pure in quality for it is the Reality.

The voice of the *lama* tells the departed one that these pleasant dream images are actually an ambush. They will entice him away and prevent him reaching the goal of existence. He must never for a moment forget that all he sees has no reality. With each successive dream scene he will begin to see other lights, too. These will be less brilliant, less pure, but often, for that reason, more tempting to the beholder whose mind is swayed by the desires and attachments of sentient existence.

The temptation to follow these false, alluring lights must be firmly resisted, however, for they lead to one or the other of many *lokas* in the subtle planes, or else to a quick rebirth on earth. Praying earnestly and humbly, the soul must concentrate on the clear, pure light, the True Light. By doing so, he will merge with the Source of all, and obtain his freedom. This message is repeated again and again.

After a period of beautiful but deluding dreams, the nature of the scene changes completely. In Tibetan imagery the "wrathful deities" begin to appear, and these are terrifying. But again the departed soul is reminded that the pageant before his eyes has no reality. It is only a projection from his own psychic head center. He is also told that, in the deepest sense, the wrathful figures threatening him are the same peaceful deities of the earlier scenes in reverse. It is as if the love and peace of the spiritual heart have been turned to hate and conflict by the intellect. Heart unites, mind divides.

If the departed soul can overcome his terror and horror at what he sees, understand it for what it actually is, and stand fast courageously, he still has a very good chance of liberation from the phenomenal worlds. But he must make an all-out effort to counter the menace, not by fleeing from it, but by realizing its dream nature and reaching, with one-pointed concentration, towards the Clear Light beyond it. If he can manage to do this during the frightful nightmare, the dreamer will immediately awake to blissful Reality.

The wise advice in the Tibetan script is valuable for all people. All cultures have frightening, hostile figures in their traditional teachings about the after-death scenes. Thought-forms of these that appear to the departed soul should be understood and treated for what they are: merely "such stuff as dreams are made of." By doing so, we will escape from the

restricting *karma* inherent in our own ideological
backgrounds, and reach enlightenment.

Following the private nightmare stage, for the
many who do not act on the *lama's* advice, there is
the Judgement. This is a common feature of all doctrines — found in the Bible, the Koran, *The Egyptian
Book of the Dead*, Swedenborg, Plato, occult teachings
and modern psychic research. The symbols and
nature of the judgement drama differ, depending on
different cultures, and the reach of individual understanding in matters of the spirit. But the purpose is
the same: the future progress and destiny of the soul.

In the Tibetan version the main symbol of the
review is the "Mirror of *Karma*." This brings all that
was hidden in the person's life into the open for
divine judgement. But, the Tibetan script teaches, as
psychic research confirms, that this is really a search-
ing self-review. The voice of the reading *lama* tells
the person that all the elements he is witnessing are
within himself, that the figures in the ominous drama
are his own mental projections. In reality, the individual's Divine Self is scrutinizing and passing judgement on the performance of the personality It
projected to live the recent life under review.

After the judgement there will normally be punishment and suffering for evils done. This is *karmic*
and part of the learning process. Yet, even at this late
stage, the individual has the opportunity to rise
above the dictates of his own *karma*. As Sai Baba
teaches today, *karma* can be erased by complete surrender to the Divine.*

The soul is now instructed by the *lama* to meditate,

---

*According to Theosophy, *karma* cannot be erased,
though it can be influenced by subsequent actions and
mitigated by the way one meets it. — ED.

to pray to the Compassionate One, or, if he prefers, to his own guardian deity. Fervent prayer, devotion and surrender to God will help him rise above his *karmic* fate.

Even if he is not able to reach liberation by such spiritual endeavors, he may avoid slipping down into some miserable hellish state, or a quick, unhappy rebirth on earth. He must feel strong revulsion about returning to earth, or going to one of the undesirable places. He must yearn for the paradise realms and concentrate with all his strength on reaching them. Apparently, the intensity of his longing and will power, helped by his prayers, plays an important part in saving him even now, before his fate is sealed for another long stretch of time.

Though help and advice are given by the *lama* all along the line, many souls will fail to benefit from them. Perhaps their veil of ignorance is too thick; perhaps they do not hear or understand the *lama's* instructions; perhaps their sentient desires are too strong. In any case, they turn away from the Clear Light. Maybe they were drawn to the happy, pleasant scenes in the first dream. Or, terrified by the nightmare, they tried to flee the menacing figures — pursued, it seemed, by the Furies. But these were in fact only their own subconscious terrors and guilt complexes.

They may try to escape the Furies by diving into the sheltering womb of Mother Earth — into any waiting womb, whether human or animal. Thus, blind fear is one cause of a speedy reincarnation. Others are sensual desires and strong earthly attachments.

But whatever the motive, a hasty rebirth without discrimination is bad. It will most likely lead to a life in circumstances and conditions that are little, if any, better than hell.

The Tibetan *lamas* advise the soul to wait, be circumspect, choose carefully and with due thought an environment conducive to a happy life. The wealth or status of a couple will not necessarily insure a progressive, useful life for their offspring. Choose, instead, a family with high spiritual values, providing good opportunities for advancement towards life's true goal. When the best possible family has been selected, and the time for rebirth has come, pray for divine blessings on the parents as you enter the womb of your next earthly mother. This lamaic advice is applicable whether it's the fate of the soul to be reborn from Bardo, or later, from one of the other subtle planes.

If the individual soul is not reborn speedily on earth, or into one of the subtle *lokas*, be they heavenly or hellish, he will inevitably stay on for a period in the intermediate world of Bardo. Then, even after he awakes from his private nightmare, he may encounter some fearful sights and sounds. These again are only illusions — the effects of his vices when living in the human world. Evil, cruel, self-centered ways of life create such unpleasant hallucinations, and also the obsession that all the other Bardo beings he meets are his enemies.

On the other hand, people who have accumulated sufficient merit on earth will experience various delightful pleasures and much happiness in higher regions of Bardo. These regions evidently correspond with some intermediate subdivisions of the astral plane, according to Theosophical classification. Here the dwellers find themselves with powers they never had and would have thought miraculous while living in this world. As described in other sources of occult knowledge, the Tibetan text explains that the dwellers have bodies which can pass through earthly solids; they can travel in a moment to any place, however far, without any power save the power of thought to propel them. Furthermore, their senses seem more clear and keen than they were on earth. Around them are people of similar interests and knowledge to their own, with whom they communicate by telepathic powers.

The light from this region is not from sun or stars, but is the astral light that is universally diffused throughout the ether. It resembles the twilight of earth, yet is quite bright enough for the keen sight of the dwellers here.

Some there are who, living lives of ease and pleasure in this astral state, want to stay on indefinitely. Others get the false idea that it is a fixed state of existence, that it is, in fact, the only spiritual world.

The *Bardo Thodöl*, however, advises that whether the state of existence is pleasant, painful or indifferent, the individual should never accept it as real. He should know it to be just a transitory creation of the collective mind. He should meditate on the Compassionate One, or on his own spiritual teacher, and in all ways continue striving to reach the Reality beyond the phenomena.

The essence of the Tibetan teachings found in their *Book of the Dead* may be stated as follows. For the majority of people the immediate after-death experience is but a continuation, under changed conditions, of life on earth. But, like this world itself, the subtle planes of Bardo, heaven, hell and other places, have no existence save in the deluded mortal minds of the beings who perceive them. All the phenomenal, seemingly real, systems are, therefore, in the final analysis, unreal. The causes of their apparent reality, and of our existence therein, are desire, thirst for sensation, karmic propensities, and the error made by our highly restricted state of consciousness, with its blinkered senses, and the distorted mental outlook created thereby. Such limiting factors apply in different degrees on all planes — physical and psychic.

Enlightenment, or the vision of the Whole, results from a realization of the illusory nature of all phenomenal existence. Such Truth-realization may be achieved in this human world; in fact, the purpose of human birth is to reach that realization. For the many who do not, the Tibetan manual for the dying and the dead informs its listeners, and us, that another great opportunity exists at the time of death. This is, perhaps, the greatest value of death; it is a hiatus, a junction where the train of consciousness is changing from the lines of earth to the lines of the next journey. Before it gets set on those new lines, and engrossed in the scenes of the next dream journey, there is a break where all dream journeys may be left behind, and the soul may soar upward to the radiant divine light. If this chance is missed, realization is still possible from Bardo, and from some of the other realms to which the soul may go.

For reaching enlightenment from any place, essentials are training in the control of the thinking process, and in the concentration of the mind. Such training can best be had in this world under an enlightened *guru*, or teacher.

Until final liberation is reached, rebirth on earth from some subtle plane, either Bardo or one of the paradise or hell regions, is inevitable. Hence death follows birth, and birth death, unceasingly, for the soul until it wins *nirvana* — the Spiritual Home, the state of eternal bliss, beyond all heavens, hells and worlds.

It is the noble purpose of *The Tibetan Book of the Dead* to guide the living, the dying and the dead towards an instant achievement of the blessedness and bliss desired, either consciously or subconsciously, by all people.

8
Summing Up

The thing we might ask ourselves now is what agreement or disagreement do we find in all the evidence that has come to us from so many widely scattered points in geography, history and prehistory. Is there a good case for life after death and, if so, what kind of a life is it compared with the life we know here?

All the teachings, from religions, spiritual philosophy and occult traditions, agree on one point — the vital point — there is life after death. This fact is supported by the evidence of modern psychic research, both inside and outside research organizations, though most researchers agree that it cannot be proved by the rigid methods of modern science.

But the evidence is surely overwhelming. Those who refuse stubbornly to accept the concept of continuing life beyond the grave are either prejudiced or are relying entirely on the five senses, known to be inadequate and misleading in the deeper questions of life. The senses are blinkers, concentrating but limiting the view.

There are, moreover, some striking features of the after-life scene on which most of the evidence is in agreement. One is that immediately following death, we will be much the same as before it. The loss of the physical body will not be noticed as we have another body that seems to be the same. As the actual transition from this world to that is swift and painless, we may find it hard to realize that we are "dead."

Another point of agreement is that soon, if not immediately after the transition, we will be met by what one writer calls the "honorary guard," whose job it is to help us understand our situation and guide us to our immediate destination. These helpers may be in the form of "dead" relatives or friends, a spiritual preceptor still living, or a great religious figure of our culture.

Another common factor in all the evidence is the Divine Judgement. This is understood by students of modern psychic science — in agreement with the Ancient Wisdom teachings — to be a Self-judgement. The Self of each of us is in reality one with God, so in this sense it could be called a divine judgement. Some may experience an outside judge figure as part of the scene. Others may be aware that their divine Selves are judging the recent performance of the personality on the stage of earth.

Whatever form the judgement drama takes, it will be for most a painful experience. Looking at the scenes of our past as they come vividly before us, we will inevitably feel deep regret, sorrow, repugnance for some of the things we did and said during our years on earth. Yet, though painful, it will be a salutary experience to review our lives from the higher, wiser perspective. From it valuable lessons will be learned for our future progress.

It is inevitable that a period of suffering must come as a result of wrong thinking and wrong living. Some of that suffering will probably take place during life on earth while, after death, the place of suffering may be called hell, or the lower astral, or by some other name. The essential lessons to be learned from the purgatorial, or hellish, conditions may take only a short time for some and centuries for others. But the weight of evidence is against the doctrine of eternal suffering for the soul.

The idea expressed by Swedenborg that man casts himself into hell seems sound. Man's own inclinations and desires take him there after death, as indeed they do before death. And he will remain there until he learns that uncontrolled passions and desires bring much more pain and torment than the illusory pleasure they seem to offer. When purified in fires of suffering the soul emerges to a better state of being.

The heavens are there, too, in all the varied teachings. Research supports the concept, for though mediumistic communications usually come from the astral levels, most of the communicators are aware of the more spiritual realms beyond. Their expectation is to move on to those realms in due course. In the felicitous heavens, it is taught, you reap the happy results of your good thoughts and actions on earth.

But there are different levels and locales in those regions known as the heavens. Depending on the life one has lived and the state of one's soul, the individual may spend a short time in one of those "many mansions," or perhaps thousands of years, as we measure time. But, time being more psychological than chronological in those regions, we do not know how long it may seem to the denizens of heaven. Yet, except in the seventh or highest heaven, no one is there for eternity. When Jesus spoke of eternity in heaven, he, no doubt, was referring to the highest heaven, called by some masters, "beyond the heavens."

In the subtle worlds of the astral and heaven planes

the residents follow their natures, which usually is to do some kind of creative work. They are not forced to work in order to live as we are here, but their natural inclination is generally towards keeping occupied. When here we do sometimes work for pleasure, and not through compulsion, we call it a hobby. Perhaps they think of all their activities in that way.

All the verdicts agree that souls have greatly enhanced powers when the confines of the gross body have been left behind. Some of the powers that come naturally in the realms of subtle nature are telepathy, clairvoyance, the power to travel instantaneously from place to place, the power to mold by thought and will the subtle matter of the region into any object desired. Here on earth we do the same thing by thought and will, plus muscle and machine power. The matter there is much more responsive to the powers of consciousness alone. So muscular and mechanical forces are not necessary. It can be seen, then, that work to acquire dwelling places, clothing, food, means of travel, and so on, is not necessary over there.

There are, however, some differences we note in the reports from the psychic explorers of the undiscovered country. These concern mainly the divisions of that country. The Theosophists, we saw, divide it into two main planes, each with seven subdivisions. The Rosicrucians talk of twelve "mansions." Swedenborg saw three main areas, each divided into three sections. The Hindus teach that there are fourteen main planes for the soul's existence before its final mergence with the Divine. And within each of these are many different regions. Roman Catholics name three after-death places, and the Protestants only two: heaven and hell.

These divisions result from information gathered

from two main sources: incarnate clairvoyant explorers and discarnate spirits. The former, by the very nature of human consciousness, and the limitations of embodied psychic senses, can at best catch only glimpses of the vast and complex territories. What they do observe they classify according to their own understanding, which is always conditioned. There are thus variations in the depth of penetration according to clairvoyant development, and variations in classifications according to cultural background. Furthermore, the fact that one zone merges into another, with no clear cut boundary (a point on which all agree) is conducive to differing classifications.

The discarnate spirits, whose voices we hear through mediums, have certainly not had an overall God's eye view of the undiscovered country. Each is reporting from his own corner of it. Usually this is situated in the lower or middle regions of the astral. Such psychic reporters generally are aware of regions beyond their own. But they have no knowledge about the number of areas outside their own, or the nature of life in them.

Moreover, if some better informed, more advanced entity descends from higher levels to communicate, his mental vibrations must necessarily be lowered to meet those of the medium concerned. Consequently, a great deal of his knowledge cannot be brought through his lowered state of consciousness. He would thus not be able to give a comprehensive picture of the undiscovered country, whatever his knowledge might be.

So the variations in the psychographical divisions need not trouble us at all. Like the variations in the early maps of little known areas of our physical world, they prove nothing more than the difficulties of exploration.

Hence, though the Bard's "undiscovered country" has been discovered as surely as Columbus discovered America, many mysteries still lie beyond its borders. Time and persistent pioneer efforts may change this situation to some extent. We will, it is hoped, learn more of the places to which we are all heading. But no doubt some mysteries will remain for eternity's solution. Our human consciousness, in the words of St. Paul, sees only through a glass darkly.

We must, therefore, strive to keep open minds on the question of what to expect when we cross the border. There is a grave danger in having rigid, inflexible ideas about these matters. Very strong beliefs, held here for a long time, can come into thought-form existence there. Fanatical believers in traditional hells and heavens, for instance, may move into thought-forms of such places, and live there for shorter or longer periods. But their hallucinatory dreams will evaporate with time, and conditions true to the astral system of reality will in the end prevail.

A happier state of existence after death awaits those who pass on with bright faith and high hopes, but without fixed ideas. They will not be upset by surprises in store, nor will they become set in the concrete of their own biased, fanatical beliefs.

Indeed, most of the great spiritual teachers say little or nothing about the planes of phenomenal existence beyond death. Jesus Christ taught practically nothing on the subject. Nor does Sai Baba say much about it. Both want us to make the great leap from the bondage of earth directly to divine freedom. Jesus called this freedom eternal heaven; Sai Baba calls it *moksha*, or union with God. Both are talking about the same thing.

But though many people are urged to do so, few

will be able to make this giant leap. The vast majority will find themselves after death somewhere in the intermediate planes. It is a good thing, therefore, to have a guidebook, however sketchy, to help us find our way in the new land. Of course, like all guide-books, it will fall short of the reality, leaving out many details, and proving incorrect in others. Still, if we remember that it is only a guidebook, concocted from limited information, it will, I feel sure, be of real practical use.

Apart from the actual reality of life after death, the mass of evidence agrees on another point: that living a good life here ensures a good transition and happy hereafter. This follows from the great Law of Com-pensation, the *Karmic* law, which states that as we sow so we reap. If we sow the seeds of hate, greed, selfishness and the like, we will surely reap a harvest of suffering somewhere in the life to come.

On the other hand, if we live closer to our higher natures, to which belong the positive emotions of love, compassion, unselfishness and the rest, we will make the great transition without the fight and fear that mar it. Then, though there still may be a period of after-death purgation, we will pass sooner to the higher levels of happiness and felicity.

A good life, an easy death, followed by a happy life in heaven is certainly a true and worthwhile for-mula. But there is something even better for which all can strive. The orthodox religions, while setting good standards of morals and ethics, do not reveal the true purpose of life or the right goal for man. The highest goal they set is the attainment of some kind of heaven, and the main purpose in life is to live so as to reach that goal. Moreover, the religions and philosophies of the West do not lead us to a true discrimination between the real and the unreal, between the eternal spirit and the mortal bodies. In fact, some philosophies, even some religions, teach that the body is the only reality.

Western religious thought needs an infusion of Vedantic, or *yogic*, philosophy to give it breadth and depth of understanding. The height and practical value of such philosophy is seen in the lives and deaths of great *yogis* and saints. Fully aware that the body is only a temporary garment, and that the true Self cannot be killed, they live lives of happiness and fulfilment. Their efforts are not towards piling up wealth or acquiring fame, those flickering shadows that pass with time, but towards reaching life's highest goal — eternal union with the Divine.

They know when the time has arrived to cast off the physical body, and they do so voluntarily and consciously. This is the ideal kind of death. There is none of the fear and struggle, none of the lingering illness, awaiting the unknown moment when death will strike. The *yogi* knows when the hour is approaching for his departure. He probably informs one or two of his disciples in advance, and they will be present to witness the event, and do whatever is required for the disposal of the cast-off body. The only sorrow in the event is that felt by the disciples because they will no longer have contact with their Master through his physical vehicle. They know, however, that he is still very much alive and, if necessary, will help and guide them from another plane of existence.

Illustrating still more the role played by the body as only a temporary dwelling, some great *yogis* and saints leave it for periods of time before their final departure. Such periods may vary from hours to days.

When Sai Baba was living at Shirdi, in India, for

example, he decided to leave his body for three days. The year was 1886, and Baba's only disciple at that time was a village goldsmith named Bhagat Mahalsapathy. To him Baba said, "Bhagat, look after this body for three days. I am going to Allah [God]. If I do not return, then get it buried at that place — near the sacred *gode neem* tree."

Baba left his body and his disciple guarded it. When officers, including the village elder, held an inquest over the body, declared it dead, and wanted it to be buried, Mahalsapathy, with the help of others, stoutly opposed this proposal. They were able to hold out against the officials until Baba came back to his body after the three days. He lived in it for another thirty-two years, set afoot the great Sai movement, and took his final departure from that particular physical form in 1918.

Sai Baba is one of those Great Beings who, though completely liberated from the bonds of the phenomenal worlds and belonging to the highest Godhead, remain, through their compassion, in touch with the bond-slave souls on earth. I once asked Satya Sai Baba where he had been and what he had been doing in the eight years between casting off his body at Shirdi and putting on a new one in Puttaparthi in 1926. "I was here near the earth," he said, "doing what I am doing now, helping people."

The fact that he did take another body, and says he will even take a third one eventually, to complete his work, indicates that to bring supreme *avataric* help to the sons of earth, the Helper needs an earthly body.

The lessons we learn from the lives of such Great Ones is that we should set our sights higher than the heaven planes, where "scenes of bliss pass as a phantom by."

Through right studies and right living, through prayer and meditation, we should get our feet firmly on the spiritual path that will lead us beyond the heavens to the eternal land that is nowhere yet everywhere, the Divine Ground of our own Being.

Suggested Reading

Barrett, Sir William, *Deathbed Visions* (London, Methuen, 1926)

Barker, A. T., comp.,*The Mahatma Letters to A. P. Sinnett* (Rider & Co.)

Crookall, Robert, *The Supreme Adventure* (London, James Clarke, 1961)

De Groot, J. J. M., *The Religious System of China*

Diwaker, R. R., *Mahayogi Sri Aurobindo* (Bombay, Bharatiya Vidya Bhavan, 1967)

Dowding, Lord, *The Dark Star* (London, Museum Press Ltd., 1951)

Delacour, Jean-Baptiste, *Glimpses of the Beyond* (published in Germany, 1973; English translation in 1974)

Frazer, Sir James G., *The Golden Bough* (Macmillan, 1922)

Head, J. & Cranston, S. L. (Eds), *Reincarnation: The Phoenix Fire Mystery* (New York, Julian Press/ Crown Publishers Inc., 1977)

Kübler-Ross, Elisabeth, *Death: the Final Stage of Growth* (Prentice-Hall, 1975)

Leadbeater, C. W., *The Life After Death* (Theosophical Publishing House, 1912)

Leadbeater, C. W., *The Other Side of Death* (Theosophical Publishing Society, 1904)

Leadbeater, C. W., various volumes on the astral & devachanic planes

Modi, Jivanji Jamshedji, *The Religious Ceremonies and Customs of the Parsees* (Bombay, British India Press, 1922)

Mbiti, John S., *African Religions and Philosophy* (London, Heinemann Education Books Ltd., 1969)

Moody, Dr. Raymond, Jr., *Life After Life* (1975)

Moody, Dr. Raymond, Jr., *Reflections on Life After Life* (New York, Mockingbird/Bantam)

Osis, Karlis, *Deathbed Observations by Physicians and Nurses* (New York, Parapsychology Foundation Inc., 1961)

Osis, K. & Haraldsson, E., "Deathbed Observations by Physicians and Nurses: a Cultural Survey" (*The Journal of the American Society for Psychical Research*,

Reisner, George Andrew, *The Egyptian Conception of Immortality* (Constable, 1912)

Radhakrishnan, S., *Indian Philosophy*, 2 volumes (London, George Allen & Unwin Ltd.)

Ryall, Edward, *Born Twice: Total Recall of a Seventeenth Century Life* (New York, Harper & Row)

Roberts, Jane, *Seth Speaks* (New Jersey, Prentice-Hall)

Sivananda, Swami, *What Becomes of the Soul After Death* (Sivanandanagar, Uttar Pradesh, India, Divine Life Society, 1972)

Wallis-Budge, E. A., *Book of the Dead, the Papyrus of Ani*

Yogananda, Paramahansa, *Autobiography of a Yogi* (Rider & Co.)

Index

Advaita, 159
African societies, 23
angels, Swedenborg on, 127
Ani, 99
Arnold, Matthew, *Empedocles on Etna*, 162
Arnold, Sir Edwin, *The Light of Asia*, 166
Asclepius, 31
astral, body, 14, 92, 94, 100-101; plane, 98, 99, 100, 110, 130; sub-planes, 99, 100, 102, 124; dweller(s), 101, 102, corpse, 105; permanent atom, 106; vehicle of lower desires, 133; entities, 133. *See also* Paradise
atom, 20; as discrete orders of particles, 118
Aurobindo, Sri, 15, 16
Australian Blacks, 22
Avichi, 103

ba, 26
Bardo, 174, 176-178; intermediate world of, 185
Bardo Thodöl, 173. *See also Tibetan Book of the Dead*
Barrett, Sir William, 75-76
Besant, Annie, 96, 97, 103, 106, 115; on communication through mediums, 135-136

Bhagavad Gita, 163
Bhuvarloka, 161
Bible, the, 9-18
Blavatsky, H. P., 132; *The Secret Doctrine*, 20, 97, 115, 116; on the human compound, 130; on séances, 134-135
body, resurrected, 8; natural, 14; spiritual, 14; causal, 110. *See also* astral body
Brahma, 17
Brahma Sutras, 159
Brahman, 160, 165-167
Broad, C. D., 62
Brookes-Smith, Colin, 64
Budge, E. A. Wallis, *Egyptian Book of the Dead*, 12

Cathar(s), 90-91
Causal body, 110
Cayce, Edward, 101
Chaffin Will Case, 57-58
Chinese, primitive, 10
Christ, 105, 108, 156; concept, 168
Christian Science, 168-173
Churches' Fellowship for Psychical and Spiritual Studies, 6
churches, mainline, 5; *See also* Protestant Church(es); Roman Catholic Church
circumstantial evidence, 63

clairvoyant explorers, 193
coma, 93
consciousness, 99; super-
    normal, 97; level of, 105;
    causal, 108; creates
    form, 152
controls, 59
Cosmic Egg, 161-162
Cowan, Walter, 84, 86-88
Crookall, Robert, 91-93, 105,
    131; on spirit communica-
    tions, 142-144, 146; on
    ghosts, 145
Crookes, Sir William, 64-72
cross-correspondence(s), 60,
    61, 62, 64

Daniel, Book of, 10
Dante, *The Divine
    Comedy*, 95
Darwin, Charles, 55, 66
David-Neel, Alexandra, 177
Dawa-Samdup, Lama
    Kazi, 174
death, father's, 47; mother's,
    48, 51; -bed visions, 73-
    79; after- experiences,
    79-88; past lives, 88-89;
    near-, 178
deGroot, J. J. M., *The Religious
    System of China*, 10
deities, peaceful, 181;
    wrathful, 182
Demeter, 38-40
devachan, 105-108
devas, 127; rupa, 115
discarnate person, 53
Divine Mind, 15, 16; man
    as, 169

Diwaker, R. R., 16
*Doctrine in the Church of
    England*, 5
Dowding, Lord, 147
dream, as existence, 170
Dvaita, or dualist, philosophy,
    167

Ear of Dionysius, 61
ectoplasm, 50, 71
Eddy farmhouse, 144
Eddy, Mary Baker, 168-173
Edwards, Harry, 148
Egyptians, prehistoric, 25
Eighth Sphere, 103
elementals, 134; artificial, 133
Eleusis, 38-39
Elysium, 28
enlightenment, 187
Er, 32-36
eternity, 158
ethereal double, 92
etheric vehicle, 93, 94
Evans, Frederick, 144-145
Evans-Wentz, T. W., 174
evolution, man's, 15; the
    soul's, 164
extrasensory, perception, 22;
    powers, 59; Swedenborg's,
    120

fate, 37
fear of the dead, 22
fire, Stockholm, 120-121
Fletcher, John, 111-112
Frazer, Sir James, 21
fundamentalist doctrines, 1

Garden of Eden, 4
Gardner, E. L., 115, 116

Gehenna, 10
ghosts, 116; *See also*
    Crookall, Robert
Giri, Yukteswar, 101, 103, 104
Gorrell, Hank, 44
Greek Meltic Poets, 61
Guirdham, Arthur, 90
Gurney, Edmund, 60
Guttierez, Vergillo, 150

Hades, 10, 27; King, 38-39
Hand, Bill, 43
Haraldsson, Erlendur, 73,
    74, 78
heaven, 4, 6, 7, 12, 33, 104;
    world, 107; seventh, 108;
    unselfish life of, 125;
    Swedenborg, 127; work in,
    128; children in, 128;
    marriage in, 128; comes to
    an end, 158; as unalloyed
    happiness, 163; different
    levels, 191; creative work
    in, 192
hell(s), 7, 12, 102, 104, 114;
    Swedenborg's, 126; in
    Christian Science, 171;
    man casts himself into, 191
Herodotus, 38
Higher Self, 93, 105
Hindu teachings, on life after
    death, 164
Hiranyaloka, 104
Hislop, John, 84-85
Hodson, Geoffrey, 96; on
    shells and shades, 137-138
Huxley, Thomas, 66
Hypnos, 27
hypnotic regression, 88

intermediate world(s), 130
intervals between births, 115
Isaiah, 10

Jesus, 12, 13; resurrected,
    14, 16
judgment, 4, 5, 93, 124; final,
    6, 8; self, 83; Tibetan, 183;
    divine, 190. *See also* review
Jung, Carl, 175

ka, 26
Kant, Immanuel, 120, 122
karma, evil, 104; group or
    national, 107; law of, 126;
    restricting, 183; mirror
    of, 183
karmic debts, 109; laws, 110
Kingdom of God, 16
Kipling, Rudyar, 109
Koot Hoomi, Master, 103, 106,
    116; Mahatma, 135
Krishna, Lord, 163
Kübler-Ross, Elisabeth, 80

Lachesis, 34
Law of Parsimony, 56, 57
law, karmic, 195
Leadbeater, C. W., 96, 97, 100,
    103, 115; on causal level,
    108; communication
    through mediums, 135; on
    spiritualism, 136-137;
    clairvoyance of, 137
Leonard, Mrs. Osborne, 144
Lewis, H. Spencer, *Mansions
    of the Soul,* 113, 114
Liberal Catholic, Church, 97
light(s), clear, 177-179, 182;

Being of, 82; false, 181; astral, 186

living dead, the, 23

Lodge, Sir Oliver, 69

loka(s), 115, 161-163; as Divine Consciousness, 162

London Dialectical Society, 66

love, 127-128

Madhava, 159, 167

Mahatma Letters, The, 103

mahatmas, 96, 97. *See also* Koot Hoomi

Mary Magdalene, 13

Massey, C. C., 67

materialism, 19

matter, 19, 98, 118; mental, 105; ethereal, 110

Mbiti, John S., *African Religions and Philosophy,* 24

medium(s), 49-50, 57; genuine and cheating, 132; aura, 134; mind of, 146; Seth on messages through, 154

mediumistic healing of the sick, 148

mental plane(s), 99, 105, 110; sub-plane(s), 99, 104-105; parts of, 130

Moody, Raymond, 80-81

mummifying the body, 12

mummy, 26

Murphy, Gardner, 60

Myers, Frederick W. H., 59-60

Mysteries, the, 37-41

Nachiketas, 156-159

nature spirits, 134

Nero, 38

New Testament, 12-13

Newton, Isaac, 118

nirvana, 109, 166, 176, 187

Novak, Anne, 51-54

Olcott, H. S., 132

Olympus, 28

Osiris, 25-26; body, 26

Osis, Karlis, 73, 78; *Deathbed Observations by Physicians and Nurses,* 73

oversoul, 113

paradise, or the higher astral, 143

Paul, St., 14, 129

Perkins, James, 96

Persephone, 38-40

Philippine healers, 148-151

physical world, 98

Piddington, J. E., 62

Pitriloka, 163

pitris, 163

plan, evolutionary, 109

plane(s), astral, 98-100, 110, 130; mental, 99, 105, 110, 130; causal, 105

Plato, 28, 31-32; *Phaedrus,* 41; *The Republic,* 32

pomegranate, 40

Powell, Arthur E., 96

prayer, 8

Pretaloka, 162

previous lives, 86

primitive peoples, 21-22. *See also* Chinese, primitive

Proclus, 41

Protestant church(es), 1, 4

psychic investigations, 66; -surgery, 149-150
Psychic Research Society, 49
Puranas, 161
purgatory, 7, 12, 114
Pythagoras, 40

Quarles, Francis, xi

Ram, N. Sri, 96
Ramanuja, 159, 166
rebirth, 110, 187; modus operandi, 109; cycle of, 115. *See also* reincarnation
redemption, final, 127
reincarnating entity, 110
reincarnation, 36; Swedenborg found no clues, 129; in Vedanta, 161; speedy, 184. *See also* rebirth
repentance, 12
resurrection, 3, 4, 10, 124; of the natural body, 10; of the physical body, 13; Christ's, 15; Egyptian, 25; Swedenborg, 124
resuscitation, 80
review, 87, 93, 124; life, 83; Seth on, 153. *See also* judgment
River of Forgetfulness, 36-37, 110
Roberts, Jane, 152
Roman Catholic Church, 6-8; on spiritualism, 138
Rosicrucian concepts, 113-116; teachings on spiritualism, 140-141
Royal Society, 67

Ryall, Edward, 111-112; *Born Twice—Total Recall of a Seventeenth Century Life,* 112

Sai Baba, 85-87, 107; on the nature of man, 160; on moksha, 194; leaving his body, 196-197
Sai Baba, Satya, 19, 197
Sambhava, Padma, 174
Saul, King, 145
Scatcherd, Miss F. R., 70-71
School of the Wisdom, 95
séance, spiritualist, 134; warnings against, 146-147. *See also* Theosophy
second death, 133
selfhood, separate, 103
Seth, 152; on death, 152-154
shade(s), 105, 133-134; as vampires, 136; or senseless ghosts, 139
Shakers, 144
Shakespeare, ix
Shankara, Adi, 159, 165
shell(s), 105, 133-134; Koot Hoomi on, 135; as vampires, 136
Sheol, 10
Sidgewick, Henry, 60, 66; Eleanor, 61
silver cord, 92
Sinnett, A. P., 96
Sisson, Josephine, 149-150
Society for Psychical Research, 54-64
Socrates, 28-31, 37
soul(s), 101, 107; pure, 29; transmigration of, 30; of the

dead, 53; mansions of the, 113, 115; destiny of, 116; from God, 127; use of dreams, 140; in the heaven world, 144; Seth on, 154; has eternal existence, 167

spirit(s), 24; guardian, 29; ancestral, 21; photographs, 70, 72; communications, 134-145; discarnate, 193

Spiritualism, 55, 132-155; on angels, 127; positive aspects of, 147-151. *See also* Rosicrucian concepts

spiritualistic rescue groups, 147-148

Stevenson, Ian, 111-112

sub-planes, 105; astral, 99-100, 102, 124; mental, 99, 104-105

Svargaloka, 161

Sweden, queen of, 121-122

Swedenborg, Emmanuel, 117-130; *True Christian Religion*, 123; on resurrection, 124, *Divine Providence*, 125; on communicating with the deceased, 141-142; on communicating spirits, 146

Taimni, I. K., 96

talas, 116; as hells, 162

Tartarus, 27, 29-30, 33

Tenko-san, 156

telepathic communications, between living and dead, 141

Thanatos, 27

theologians, 5

Theosophical Society, the, 67, 132

Theosophy, 95, 99; on séances, 134

Thomas, Rev. C. Drayton, 144

thought-forms, 133, 194

Thouless, Robert, 62

Thurston, Rev. Herbert, *Spiritualism*, 138-139

Tibetan Book of the Dead, 173-188

Tibetan lamas, 139

time, 17; devachanic, 108

trishna, 109-110

Ulysses, 35

Upanishad(s), 159; Katha, 159

vajasrava, 156-159

Varley, Cromwell, 65

Vedanta, 159; Dvaita, 159; on death, 161; compared with Christian Science, 168-173

Virgil, 37

Visishtadvaita, 159

voidness, 180

Wambach, Helen, 88

witch at Endor, 145

Yama, 77, 156-159

Yogananda, Paramahansa, 104

Yogavasishta, 41

Zeus, 39

QUEST BOOKS
are published by
The Theosophical Society in America,
Wheaton, Illinois 60189-0270,
a branch of a world organization
dedicated to the promotion of the unity of
humanity and the encouragement of the study of
religion, philosophy, and science, to the end that
we may better understand ourselves and our place in
the universe. The Society stands for complete
freedom of individual search and belief.
In the Classics Series well-known
theosophical works are made
available in popular editions.
For more information
write or call.
1-708-668-1571

We publish books on:
Healing and Health ● Metaphysics and
Mysticism ● Transpersonal Psychology
Philosophy ● Religion ● Reincarnation,
Science ● Yoga and Meditation.

Other books of possible interest include:

Beyond the Post-Modern Mind *by Huston Smith*
Revised edition reviews latest ideas in science and theology.

East Meets West *edited by Rosemarie Stewart*
Our higher nature and transpersonal psychological
implications.

From Atom to Kosmos *by L. Gordon Plummer*
Astronomy's stupendous universe theory relates to mysticism.

Fullness of Human Experience *by Dane Rudhyar*
How cyclic nature of creation affects our psychic evolution.

Inner Adventures *by E. Lester Smith*
Eminent scientist probes limits of thought and intuition.

Rhythm of Wholeness *by Dane Rudhyar*
We are part and parcel of the wholeness that always is.

The Theatre of the Mind *by Henryk Skolimowski*
The scope and importance of our evolution.

Two Faces of Time *by Lawrence W. Fagg*
Comparative study of time as viewed by religion and science.

The Wholeness Principle *by Anna Lemkow*
U. N. economist shows how all life is interdependent and
unitive.

Available from:
The Theosophical Publishing House
P.O. Box 270, Wheaton, Illinois 60189-0270